We hope this script will serve you and your business well. It's not a one size fits all, but hopefully it fits most scenarios. If there's anything in the script you don't need, simply skip it. Any additional questions/answers can be written in the notes. If you'd like something custom, feel free to contact us at prowashgeorgia.us@gmail.com or find us on Facebok at ProWash Georgia. Be blessed and wash on!

© PUNKTILIOUS PLANNERS. ALL RIGHTS RESERVED. NO PART OF THIS PUBLICATION MAY BE REPRODUCED, DISTRIBUTED, OR TRANSMITTED IN ANY FORM OR BY ANY MEANS, INCLUDING PHOTOCOPYING, RECORDING, OR OTHER ELECTRONIC OR MECHANICAL METHODS, WITHOUT PRIOR WRITTEN PERMISSION OF THE PUBLISHER, EXCEPT IN THE CASE OF BRIEF QUOTATIONS EMBODIED IN CRITICAL REVIEWS AND CERTAIN OTHER NONCOMMERCIAL USES PERMITTED BY COPYRIGHT LAW.

Date:
Name (first & last):
Email Address:
Mobile Phone Number:
Preferred contact method (call, text, email)
How did you hear about us? (Facebook, Google, flyer, friend, etc.)

Property address: Billing address (if different):
Address: Address:
Apt, Suite, Bldg, etc: Apt, Suite, Bldg, etc:
City, State, Zip: City, State, Zip:

What service do you need?

☐ Flat surfaces:
Type of material (concrete, pavers, wood, etc.)
If concrete, how old?
Any oil or rust stains we should know about?

☐ House Wash:
Type of material (brick, vinyl, stucco, wood, etc.)
Square footage of home/building:
How many stories?
If cleaning windows, how many?
If cleaning gutters, how old?

☐ Roof Wash:
Type of material (shingle, tile, metal, wood, etc.)
Anything on the roof? (satellite dish, solar panels, etc.)

☐ Do you have a running water hookup onsite for a water hose?
☐ Does anything need to be moved? (cars, furniture, plants, decorations, etc.) If we are responsible for moving items and putting them back, we may charge a fee.
☐ Do you have any pets? Inform pet owners they should keep pets indoors or away from work area until everything is dry. If pet safe products are preferred, there will be an upcharge and deposit required.
☐ Do you live on/near any bodies of water? (lake, river, etc.)
☐ Do I need a gate code to access the property?

Best day/time for service
Estimate: $
Notes:
_____
_____
_____
_____

Date:
Name (first & last):
Email Address:
Mobile Phone Number:
Preferred contact method (call, text, email)
How did you hear about us? (Facebook, Google, flyer, friend, etc.)

Property address:	Billing address (if different):
Address:	Address:
Apt, Suite, Bldg, etc:	Apt, Suite, Bldg, etc:
City, State, Zip:	City, State, Zip:

What service do you need?

☐ Flat surfaces:
Type of material (concrete, pavers, wood, etc.)
If concrete, how old?
Any oil or rust stains we should know about?

☐ House Wash:
Type of material (brick, vinyl, stucco, wood, etc.)
Square footage of home/building:
How many stories?
If cleaning windows, how many?
If cleaning gutters, how old?

☐ Roof Wash:
Type of material (shingle, tile, metal, wood, etc.)
Anything on the roof? (satellite dish, solar panels, etc.)

☐ Do you have a running water hookup onsite for a water hose?
☐ Does anything need to be moved? (cars, furniture, plants, decorations, etc.) If we are responsible for moving items and putting them back, we may charge a fee.
☐ Do you have any pets? Inform pet owners they should keep pets indoors or away from work area until everything is dry. If pet safe products are preferred, there will be an upcharge and deposit required.
☐ Do you live on/near any bodies of water? (lake, river, etc.)
☐ Do I need a gate code to access the property?

Best day/time for service
Estimate: $
Notes:
_____
_____
_____
_____
_____

Date:
Name (first & last):
Email Address:
Mobile Phone Number:
Preferred contact method (call, text, email)
How did you hear about us? (Facebook, Google, flyer, friend, etc.)

Property address:	Billing address (if different):
Address:	Address:
Apt, Suite, Bldg, etc:	Apt, Suite, Bldg, etc:
City, State, Zip:	City, State, Zip:

What service do you need?

☐ Flat surfaces:
Type of material (concrete, pavers, wood, etc.)
If concrete, how old?
Any oil or rust stains we should know about?

☐ House Wash:
Type of material (brick, vinyl, stucco, wood, etc.)
Square footage of home/building:
How many stories?
If cleaning windows, how many?
If cleaning gutters, how old?

☐ Roof Wash:
Type of material (shingle, tile, metal, wood, etc.)
Anything on the roof? (satellite dish, solar panels, etc.)

☐ Do you have a running water hookup onsite for a water hose?
☐ Does anything need to be moved? (cars, furniture, plants, decorations, etc.) If we are responsible for moving items and putting them back, we may charge a fee.
☐ Do you have any pets? Inform pet owners they should keep pets indoors or away from work area until everything is dry. If pet safe products are preferred, there will be an upcharge and deposit required.
☐ Do you live on/near any bodies of water? (lake, river, etc.)
☐ Do I need a gate code to access the property?

Best day/time for service
Estimate: $
Notes:
_____
_____
_____
_____

Date:
Name (first & last):
Email Address:
Mobile Phone Number:
Preferred contact method (call, text, email)
How did you hear about us? (Facebook, Google, flyer, friend, etc.)

Property address:	Billing address (if different):
Address:	Address:
Apt, Suite, Bldg, etc:	Apt, Suite, Bldg, etc:
City, State, Zip:	City, State, Zip:

What service do you need?

☐ Flat surfaces:
Type of material (concrete, pavers, wood, etc.)
If concrete, how old?
Any oil or rust stains we should know about?

☐ House Wash:
Type of material (brick, vinyl, stucco, wood, etc.)
Square footage of home/building:
How many stories?
If cleaning windows, how many?
If cleaning gutters, how old?

☐ Roof Wash:
Type of material (shingle, tile, metal, wood, etc.)
Anything on the roof? (satellite dish, solar panels, etc.)

☐ Do you have a running water hookup onsite for a water hose?
☐ Does anything need to be moved? (cars, furniture, plants, decorations, etc.) If we are responsible for moving items and putting them back, we may charge a fee.
☐ Do you have any pets? Inform pet owners they should keep pets indoors or away from work area until everything is dry. If pet safe products are preferred, there will be an upcharge and deposit required.
☐ Do you live on/near any bodies of water? (lake, river, etc.)
☐ Do I need a gate code to access the property?

Best day/time for service
Estimate: $
Notes:
_____
_____
_____
_____
_____

Date:
Name (first & last):
Email Address:
Mobile Phone Number:
Preferred contact method (call, text, email)
How did you hear about us? (Facebook, Google, flyer, friend, etc.)

Property address:	Billing address (if different):
Address:	Address:
Apt, Suite, Bldg, etc:	Apt, Suite, Bldg, etc:
City, State, Zip:	City, State, Zip:

What service do you need?

☐ Flat surfaces:
Type of material (concrete, pavers, wood, etc.)
If concrete, how old?
Any oil or rust stains we should know about?

☐ House Wash:
Type of material (brick, vinyl, stucco, wood, etc.)
Square footage of home/building:
How many stories?
If cleaning windows, how many?
If cleaning gutters, how old?

☐ Roof Wash:
Type of material (shingle, tile, metal, wood, etc.)
Anything on the roof? (satellite dish, solar panels, etc.)

☐ Do you have a running water hookup onsite for a water hose?
☐ Does anything need to be moved? (cars, furniture, plants, decorations, etc.) If we are responsible for moving items and putting them back, we may charge a fee.
☐ Do you have any pets? Inform pet owners they should keep pets indoors or away from work area until everything is dry. If pet safe products are preferred, there will be an upcharge and deposit required.
☐ Do you live on/near any bodies of water? (lake, river, etc.)
☐ Do I need a gate code to access the property?

Best day/time for service
Estimate: $
Notes:

_____
_____
_____
_____

Date:
Name (first & last):
Email Address:
Mobile Phone Number:
Preferred contact method (call, text, email)
How did you hear about us? (Facebook, Google, flyer, friend, etc.)

Property address:	Billing address (if different):
Address:	Address:
Apt, Suite, Bldg, etc:	Apt, Suite, Bldg, etc:
City, State, Zip:	City, State, Zip:

What service do you need?

☐ Flat surfaces:
Type of material (concrete, pavers, wood, etc.)
If concrete, how old?
Any oil or rust stains we should know about?

☐ House Wash:
Type of material (brick, vinyl, stucco, wood, etc.)
Square footage of home/building:
How many stories?
If cleaning windows, how many?
If cleaning gutters, how old?

☐ Roof Wash:
Type of material (shingle, tile, metal, wood, etc.)
Anything on the roof? (satellite dish, solar panels, etc.)

☐ Do you have a running water hookup onsite for a water hose?
☐ Does anything need to be moved? (cars, furniture, plants, decorations, etc.) If we are responsible for moving items and putting them back, we may charge a fee.
☐ Do you have any pets? Inform pet owners they should keep pets indoors or away from work area until everything is dry. If pet safe products are preferred, there will be an upcharge and deposit required.
☐ Do you live on/near any bodies of water? (lake, river, etc.)
☐ Do I need a gate code to access the property?

Best day/time for service
Estimate: $
Notes:
_____
_____
_____
_____
_____

Date:
Name (first & last):
Email Address:
Mobile Phone Number:
Preferred contact method (call, text, email)
How did you hear about us? (Facebook, Google, flyer, friend, etc.)

Property address: Billing address (if different):
Address: Address:
Apt, Suite, Bldg, etc: Apt, Suite, Bldg, etc:
City, State, Zip: City, State, Zip:

What service do you need?

☐ Flat surfaces:
Type of material (concrete, pavers, wood, etc.)
If concrete, how old?
Any oil or rust stains we should know about?

☐ House Wash:
Type of material (brick, vinyl, stucco, wood, etc.)
Square footage of home/building:
How many stories?
If cleaning windows, how many?
If cleaning gutters, how old?

☐ Roof Wash:
Type of material (shingle, tile, metal, wood, etc.)
Anything on the roof? (satellite dish, solar panels, etc.)

☐ Do you have a running water hookup onsite for a water hose?
☐ Does anything need to be moved? (cars, furniture, plants, decorations, etc.) If we are responsible for moving items and putting them back, we may charge a fee.
☐ Do you have any pets? Inform pet owners they should keep pets indoors or away from work area until everything is dry. If pet safe products are preferred, there will be an upcharge and deposit required.
☐ Do you live on/near any bodies of water? (lake, river, etc.)
☐ Do I need a gate code to access the property?

Best day/time for service
Estimate: $
Notes:
_____
_____
_____
_____

Date:
Name (first & last):
Email Address:
Mobile Phone Number:
Preferred contact method (call, text, email)
How did you hear about us? (Facebook, Google, flyer, friend, etc.)

Property address:	Billing address (if different):
Address:	Address:
Apt, Suite, Bldg, etc:	Apt, Suite, Bldg, etc:
City, State, Zip:	City, State, Zip:

What service do you need?

☐ Flat surfaces:
Type of material (concrete, pavers, wood, etc.)
If concrete, how old?
Any oil or rust stains we should know about?

☐ House Wash:
Type of material (brick, vinyl, stucco, wood, etc.)
Square footage of home/building:
How many stories?
If cleaning windows, how many?
If cleaning gutters, how old?

☐ Roof Wash:
Type of material (shingle, tile, metal, wood, etc.)
Anything on the roof? (satellite dish, solar panels, etc.)

☐ Do you have a running water hookup onsite for a water hose?
☐ Does anything need to be moved? (cars, furniture, plants, decorations, etc.) If we are responsible for moving items and putting them back, we may charge a fee.
☐ Do you have any pets? Inform pet owners they should keep pets indoors or away from work area until everything is dry. If pet safe products are preferred, there will be an upcharge and deposit required.
☐ Do you live on/near any bodies of water? (lake, river, etc.)
☐ Do I need a gate code to access the property?

Best day/time for service
Estimate: $
Notes:

_____
_____
_____
_____
_____

Date:
Name (first & last):
Email Address:
Mobile Phone Number:
Preferred contact method (call, text, email)
How did you hear about us? (Facebook, Google, flyer, friend, etc.)

Property address:Billing address (if different):
Address:Address:
Apt, Suite, Bldg, etc:Apt, Suite, Bldg, etc:
City, State, Zip:City, State, Zip:

What service do you need?

☐ Flat surfaces:
Type of material (concrete, pavers, wood, etc.)
If concrete, how old?
Any oil or rust stains we should know about?

☐ House Wash:
Type of material (brick, vinyl, stucco, wood, etc.)
Square footage of home/building:
How many stories?
If cleaning windows, how many?
If cleaning gutters, how old?

☐ Roof Wash:
Type of material (shingle, tile, metal, wood, etc.)
Anything on the roof? (satellite dish, solar panels, etc.)

☐ Do you have a running water hookup onsite for a water hose?
☐ Does anything need to be moved? (cars, furniture, plants, decorations, etc.) If we are responsible for moving items and putting them back, we may charge a fee.
☐ Do you have any pets? Inform pet owners they should keep pets indoors or away from work area until everything is dry. If pet safe products are preferred, there will be an upcharge and deposit required.
☐ Do you live on/near any bodies of water? (lake, river, etc.)
☐ Do I need a gate code to access the property?

Best day/time for service
Estimate: $
Notes:
_____
_____
_____
_____

Date:
Name (first & last):
Email Address:
Mobile Phone Number:
Preferred contact method (call, text, email)
How did you hear about us? (Facebook, Google, flyer, friend, etc.)

Property address:	Billing address (if different):
Address:	Address:
Apt, Suite, Bldg, etc:	Apt, Suite, Bldg, etc:
City, State, Zip:	City, State, Zip:

What service do you need?

☐ Flat surfaces:
Type of material (concrete, pavers, wood, etc.)
If concrete, how old?
Any oil or rust stains we should know about?

☐ House Wash:
Type of material (brick, vinyl, stucco, wood, etc.)
Square footage of home/building:
How many stories?
If cleaning windows, how many?
If cleaning gutters, how old?

☐ Roof Wash:
Type of material (shingle, tile, metal, wood, etc.)
Anything on the roof? (satellite dish, solar panels, etc.)

☐ Do you have a running water hookup onsite for a water hose?
☐ Does anything need to be moved? (cars, furniture, plants, decorations, etc.) If we are responsible for moving items and putting them back, we may charge a fee.
☐ Do you have any pets? Inform pet owners they should keep pets indoors or away from work area until everything is dry. If pet safe products are preferred, there will be an upcharge and deposit required.
☐ Do you live on/near any bodies of water? (lake, river, etc.)
☐ Do I need a gate code to access the property?

Best day/time for service
Estimate: $
Notes:

_____
_____
_____
_____
_____

Date:
Name (first & last):
Email Address:
Mobile Phone Number:
Preferred contact method (call, text, email)
How did you hear about us? (Facebook, Google, flyer, friend, etc.)

Property address:	Billing address (if different):
Address:	Address:
Apt, Suite, Bldg, etc:	Apt, Suite, Bldg, etc:
City, State, Zip:	City, State, Zip:

What service do you need?

☐ Flat surfaces:
Type of material (concrete, pavers, wood, etc.)
If concrete, how old?
Any oil or rust stains we should know about?

☐ House Wash:
Type of material (brick, vinyl, stucco, wood, etc.)
Square footage of home/building:
How many stories?
If cleaning windows, how many?
If cleaning gutters, how old?

☐ Roof Wash:
Type of material (shingle, tile, metal, wood, etc.)
Anything on the roof? (satellite dish, solar panels, etc.)

☐ Do you have a running water hookup onsite for a water hose?
☐ Does anything need to be moved? (cars, furniture, plants, decorations, etc.) If we are responsible for moving items and putting them back, we may charge a fee.
☐ Do you have any pets? Inform pet owners they should keep pets indoors or away from work area until everything is dry. If pet safe products are preferred, there will be an upcharge and deposit required.
☐ Do you live on/near any bodies of water? (lake, river, etc.)
☐ Do I need a gate code to access the property?

Best day/time for service
Estimate: $
Notes:
_____
_____
_____
_____

Date:
Name (first & last):
Email Address:
Mobile Phone Number:
Preferred contact method (call, text, email)
How did you hear about us? (Facebook, Google, flyer, friend, etc.)

Property address:
Address:
Apt, Suite, Bldg, etc:
City, State, Zip:

Billing address (if different):
Address:
Apt, Suite, Bldg, etc:
City, State, Zip:

What service do you need?

☐ Flat surfaces:
Type of material (concrete, pavers, wood, etc.)
If concrete, how old?
Any oil or rust stains we should know about?

☐ House Wash:
Type of material (brick, vinyl, stucco, wood, etc.)
Square footage of home/building:
How many stories?
If cleaning windows, how many?
If cleaning gutters, how old?

☐ Roof Wash:
Type of material (shingle, tile, metal, wood, etc.)
Anything on the roof? (satellite dish, solar panels, etc.)

☐ Do you have a running water hookup onsite for a water hose?
☐ Does anything need to be moved? (cars, furniture, plants, decorations, etc.) If we are responsible for moving items and putting them back, we may charge a fee.
☐ Do you have any pets? Inform pet owners they should keep pets indoors or away from work area until everything is dry. If pet safe products are preferred, there will be an upcharge and deposit required.
☐ Do you live on/near any bodies of water? (lake, river, etc.)
☐ Do I need a gate code to access the property?

Best day/time for service
Estimate: $
Notes:

_____
_____
_____
_____
_____

Date:
Name (first & last):
Email Address:
Mobile Phone Number:
Preferred contact method (call, text, email)
How did you hear about us? (Facebook, Google, flyer, friend, etc.)

Property address:	Billing address (if different):
Address:	Address:
Apt, Suite, Bldg, etc:	Apt, Suite, Bldg, etc:
City, State, Zip:	City, State, Zip:

What service do you need?

☐ Flat surfaces:
Type of material (concrete, pavers, wood, etc.)
If concrete, how old?
Any oil or rust stains we should know about?

☐ House Wash:
Type of material (brick, vinyl, stucco, wood, etc.)
Square footage of home/building:
How many stories?
If cleaning windows, how many?
If cleaning gutters, how old?

☐ Roof Wash:
Type of material (shingle, tile, metal, wood, etc.)
Anything on the roof? (satellite dish, solar panels, etc.)

☐ Do you have a running water hookup onsite for a water hose?
☐ Does anything need to be moved? (cars, furniture, plants, decorations, etc.) If we are responsible for moving items and putting them back, we may charge a fee.
☐ Do you have any pets? Inform pet owners they should keep pets indoors or away from work area until everything is dry. If pet safe products are preferred, there will be an upcharge and deposit required.
☐ Do you live on/near any bodies of water? (lake, river, etc.)
☐ Do I need a gate code to access the property?

Best day/time for service
Estimate: $
Notes:

_____
_____
_____
_____
_____

Date:
Name (first & last):
Email Address:
Mobile Phone Number:
Preferred contact method (call, text, email)
How did you hear about us? (Facebook, Google, flyer, friend, etc.)

Property address:
Address:
Apt, Suite, Bldg, etc:
City, State, Zip:

Billing address (if different):
Address:
Apt, Suite, Bldg, etc:
City, State, Zip:

What service do you need?

☐ Flat surfaces:
Type of material (concrete, pavers, wood, etc.)
If concrete, how old?
Any oil or rust stains we should know about?

☐ House Wash:
Type of material (brick, vinyl, stucco, wood, etc.)
Square footage of home/building:
How many stories?
If cleaning windows, how many?
If cleaning gutters, how old?

☐ Roof Wash:
Type of material (shingle, tile, metal, wood, etc.)
Anything on the roof? (satellite dish, solar panels, etc.)

☐ Do you have a running water hookup onsite for a water hose?
☐ Does anything need to be moved? (cars, furniture, plants, decorations, etc.) If we are responsible for moving items and putting them back, we may charge a fee.
☐ Do you have any pets? Inform pet owners they should keep pets indoors or away from work area until everything is dry. If pet safe products are preferred, there will be an upcharge and deposit required.
☐ Do you live on/near any bodies of water? (lake, river, etc.)
☐ Do I need a gate code to access the property?

Best day/time for service
Estimate: $
Notes:

_____
_____
_____
_____
_____

Date:
Name (first & last):
Email Address:
Mobile Phone Number:
Preferred contact method (call, text, email)
How did you hear about us? (Facebook, Google, flyer, friend, etc.)

Property address:	Billing address (if different):
Address:	Address:
Apt, Suite, Bldg, etc:	Apt, Suite, Bldg, etc:
City, State, Zip:	City, State, Zip:

What service do you need?

☐ Flat surfaces:
Type of material (concrete, pavers, wood, etc.)
If concrete, how old?
Any oil or rust stains we should know about?

☐ House Wash:
Type of material (brick, vinyl, stucco, wood, etc.)
Square footage of home/building:
How many stories?
If cleaning windows, how many?
If cleaning gutters, how old?

☐ Roof Wash:
Type of material (shingle, tile, metal, wood, etc.)
Anything on the roof? (satellite dish, solar panels,etc.)

☐ Do you have a running water hookup onsite for a water hose?
☐ Does anything need to be moved? (cars, furniture, plants, decorations, etc.) If we are responsible for moving items and putting them back, we may charge a fee.
☐ Do you have any pets? Inform pet owners they should keep pets indoors or away from work area until everything is dry. If pet safe products are preferred, there will be an upcharge and deposit required.
☐ Do you live on/near any bodies of water? (lake, river, etc.)
☐ Do I need a gate code to access the property?

Best day/time for service
Estimate: $
Notes:
_____
_____
_____
_____

Date:
Name (first & last):
Email Address:
Mobile Phone Number:
Preferred contact method (call, text, email)
How did you hear about us? (Facebook, Google, flyer, friend, etc.)

Property address:	Billing address (if different):
Address:	Address:
Apt, Suite, Bldg, etc:	Apt, Suite, Bldg, etc:
City, State, Zip:	City, State, Zip:

What service do you need?

☐ Flat surfaces:
Type of material (concrete, pavers, wood, etc.)
If concrete, how old?
Any oil or rust stains we should know about?

☐ House Wash:
Type of material (brick, vinyl, stucco, wood, etc.)
Square footage of home/building:
How many stories?
If cleaning windows, how many?
If cleaning gutters, how old?

☐ Roof Wash:
Type of material (shingle, tile, metal, wood, etc.)
Anything on the roof? (satellite dish, solar panels, etc.)

☐ Do you have a running water hookup onsite for a water hose?
☐ Does anything need to be moved? (cars, furniture, plants, decorations, etc.) If we are responsible for moving items and putting them back, we may charge a fee.
☐ Do you have any pets? Inform pet owners they should keep pets indoors or away from work area until everything is dry. If pet safe products are preferred, there will be an upcharge and deposit required.
☐ Do you live on/near any bodies of water? (lake, river, etc.)
☐ Do I need a gate code to access the property?

Best day/time for service
Estimate: $
Notes:
_____
_____
_____
_____
_____

Date:
Name (first & last):
Email Address:
Mobile Phone Number:
Preferred contact method (call, text, email)
How did you hear about us? (Facebook, Google, flyer, friend, etc.)

Property address:	Billing address (if different):
Address:	Address:
Apt, Suite, Bldg, etc:	Apt, Suite, Bldg, etc:
City, State, Zip:	City, State, Zip:

What service do you need?

☐ Flat surfaces:
Type of material (concrete, pavers, wood, etc.)
If concrete, how old?
Any oil or rust stains we should know about?

☐ House Wash:
Type of material (brick, vinyl, stucco, wood, etc.)
Square footage of home/building:
How many stories?
If cleaning windows, how many?
If cleaning gutters, how old?

☐ Roof Wash:
Type of material (shingle, tile, metal, wood, etc.)
Anything on the roof? (satellite dish, solar panels, etc.)

☐ Do you have a running water hookup onsite for a water hose?
☐ Does anything need to be moved? (cars, furniture, plants, decorations, etc.) If we are responsible for moving items and putting them back, we may charge a fee.
☐ Do you have any pets? Inform pet owners they should keep pets indoors or away from work area until everything is dry. If pet safe products are preferred, there will be an upcharge and deposit required.
☐ Do you live on/near any bodies of water? (lake, river, etc.)
☐ Do I need a gate code to access the property?

Best day/time for service
Estimate: $
Notes:
_____
_____
_____
_____

Date:
Name (first & last):
Email Address:
Mobile Phone Number:
Preferred contact method (call, text, email)
How did you hear about us? (Facebook, Google, flyer, friend, etc.)

Property address:						Billing address (if different):
Address:							Address:
Apt, Suite, Bldg, etc:						Apt, Suite, Bldg, etc:
City, State, Zip:						City, State, Zip:

What service do you need?

☐ Flat surfaces:
Type of material (concrete, pavers, wood, etc.)
If concrete, how old?
Any oil or rust stains we should know about?

☐ House Wash:
Type of material (brick, vinyl, stucco, wood, etc.)
Square footage of home/building:
How many stories?
If cleaning windows, how many?
If cleaning gutters, how old?

☐ Roof Wash:
Type of material (shingle, tile, metal, wood, etc.)
Anything on the roof? (satellite dish, solar panels, etc.)

☐ Do you have a running water hookup onsite for a water hose?
☐ Does anything need to be moved? (cars, furniture, plants, decorations, etc.) If we are responsible for moving items and putting them back, we may charge a fee.
☐ Do you have any pets? Inform pet owners they should keep pets indoors or away from work area until everything is dry. If pet safe products are preferred, there will be an upcharge and deposit required.
☐ Do you live on/near any bodies of water? (lake, river, etc.)
☐ Do I need a gate code to access the property?

Best day/time for service
Estimate: $
Notes:

_____
_____
_____
_____
_____

Date:
Name (first & last):
Email Address:
Mobile Phone Number:
Preferred contact method (call, text, email)
How did you hear about us? (Facebook, Google, flyer, friend, etc.)

Property address: Billing address (if different):
Address: Address:
Apt, Suite, Bldg, etc: Apt, Suite, Bldg, etc:
City, State, Zip: City, State, Zip:

What service do you need?

☐ Flat surfaces:
Type of material (concrete, pavers, wood, etc.)
If concrete, how old?
Any oil or rust stains we should know about?

☐ House Wash:
Type of material (brick, vinyl, stucco, wood, etc.)
Square footage of home/building:
How many stories?
If cleaning windows, how many?
If cleaning gutters, how old?

☐ Roof Wash:
Type of material (shingle, tile, metal, wood, etc.)
Anything on the roof? (satellite dish, solar panels, etc.)

☐ Do you have a running water hookup onsite for a water hose?
☐ Does anything need to be moved? (cars, furniture, plants, decorations, etc.) If we are responsible for moving items and putting them back, we may charge a fee.
☐ Do you have any pets? Inform pet owners they should keep pets indoors or away from work area until everything is dry. If pet safe products are preferred, there will be an upcharge and deposit required.
☐ Do you live on/near any bodies of water? (lake, river, etc.)
☐ Do I need a gate code to access the property?

Best day/time for service
Estimate: $
Notes:

_____
_____
_____
_____

Date:
Name (first & last):
Email Address:
Mobile Phone Number:
Preferred contact method (call, text, email)
How did you hear about us? (Facebook, Google, flyer, friend, etc.)

Property address:	Billing address (if different):
Address:	Address:
Apt, Suite, Bldg, etc:	Apt, Suite, Bldg, etc:
City, State, Zip:	City, State, Zip:

What service do you need?

☐ Flat surfaces:
Type of material (concrete, pavers, wood, etc.)
If concrete, how old?
Any oil or rust stains we should know about?

☐ House Wash:
Type of material (brick, vinyl, stucco, wood, etc.)
Square footage of home/building:
How many stories?
If cleaning windows, how many?
If cleaning gutters, how old?

☐ Roof Wash:
Type of material (shingle, tile, metal, wood, etc.)
Anything on the roof? (satellite dish, solar panels, etc.)

☐ Do you have a running water hookup onsite for a water hose?
☐ Does anything need to be moved? (cars, furniture, plants, decorations, etc.) If we are responsible for moving items and putting them back, we may charge a fee.
☐ Do you have any pets? Inform pet owners they should keep pets indoors or away from work area until everything is dry. If pet safe products are preferred, there will be an upcharge and deposit required.
☐ Do you live on/near any bodies of water? (lake, river, etc.)
☐ Do I need a gate code to access the property?

Best day/time for service
Estimate: $
Notes:
_____
_____
_____
_____
_____

Date:
Name (first & last):
Email Address:
Mobile Phone Number:
Preferred contact method (call, text, email)
How did you hear about us? (Facebook, Google, flyer, friend, etc.)

Property address:	Billing address (if different):
Address:	Address:
Apt, Suite, Bldg, etc:	Apt, Suite, Bldg, etc:
City, State, Zip:	City, State, Zip:

What service do you need?

☐ Flat surfaces:
Type of material (concrete, pavers, wood, etc.)
If concrete, how old?
Any oil or rust stains we should know about?

☐ House Wash:
Type of material (brick, vinyl, stucco, wood, etc.)
Square footage of home/building:
How many stories?
If cleaning windows, how many?
If cleaning gutters, how old?

☐ Roof Wash:
Type of material (shingle, tile, metal, wood, etc.)
Anything on the roof? (satellite dish, solar panels, etc.)

☐ Do you have a running water hookup onsite for a water hose?
☐ Does anything need to be moved? (cars, furniture, plants, decorations, etc.) If we are responsible for moving items and putting them back, we may charge a fee.
☐ Do you have any pets? Inform pet owners they should keep pets indoors or away from work area until everything is dry. If pet safe products are preferred, there will be an upcharge and deposit required.
☐ Do you live on/near any bodies of water? (lake, river, etc.)
☐ Do I need a gate code to access the property?

Best day/time for service
Estimate: $
Notes:

_____
_____
_____
_____

Date:
Name (first & last):
Email Address:
Mobile Phone Number:
Preferred contact method (call, text, email)
How did you hear about us? (Facebook, Google, flyer, friend, etc.)

Property address: Billing address (if different):
Address: Address:
Apt, Suite, Bldg, etc: Apt, Suite, Bldg, etc:
City, State, Zip: City, State, Zip:

What service do you need?

☐ Flat surfaces:
Type of material (concrete, pavers, wood, etc.)
If concrete, how old?
Any oil or rust stains we should know about?

☐ House Wash:
Type of material (brick, vinyl, stucco, wood, etc.)
Square footage of home/building:
How many stories?
If cleaning windows, how many?
If cleaning gutters, how old?

☐ Roof Wash:
Type of material (shingle, tile, metal, wood, etc.)
Anything on the roof? (satellite dish, solar panels, etc.)

☐ Do you have a running water hookup onsite for a water hose?
☐ Does anything need to be moved? (cars, furniture, plants, decorations, etc.) If we are responsible for moving items and putting them back, we may charge a fee.
☐ Do you have any pets? Inform pet owners they should keep pets indoors or away from work area until everything is dry. If pet safe products are preferred, there will be an upcharge and deposit required.
☐ Do you live on/near any bodies of water? (lake, river, etc.)
☐ Do I need a gate code to access the property?

Best day/time for service
Estimate: $
Notes:

_____
_____
_____
_____
_____

Date:
Name (first & last):
Email Address:
Mobile Phone Number:
Preferred contact method (call, text, email)
How did you hear about us? (Facebook, Google, flyer, friend, etc.)

Property address:	Billing address (if different):
Address:	Address:
Apt, Suite, Bldg, etc:	Apt, Suite, Bldg, etc:
City, State, Zip:	City, State, Zip:

What service do you need?

☐ Flat surfaces:
Type of material (concrete, pavers, wood, etc.)
If concrete, how old?
Any oil or rust stains we should know about?

☐ House Wash:
Type of material (brick, vinyl, stucco, wood, etc.)
Square footage of home/building:
How many stories?
If cleaning windows, how many?
If cleaning gutters, how old?

☐ Roof Wash:
Type of material (shingle, tile, metal, wood, etc.)
Anything on the roof? (satellite dish, solar panels, etc.)

☐ Do you have a running water hookup onsite for a water hose?
☐ Does anything need to be moved? (cars, furniture, plants, decorations, etc.) If we are responsible for moving items and putting them back, we may charge a fee.
☐ Do you have any pets? Inform pet owners they should keep pets indoors or away from work area until everything is dry. If pet safe products are preferred, there will be an upcharge and deposit required.
☐ Do you live on/near any bodies of water? (lake, river, etc.)
☐ Do I need a gate code to access the property?

Best day/time for service
Estimate: $
Notes:
_____
_____
_____
_____

Date:
Name (first & last):
Email Address:
Mobile Phone Number:
Preferred contact method (call, text, email)
How did you hear about us? (Facebook, Google, flyer, friend, etc.)

Property address:
Address:
Apt, Suite, Bldg, etc:
City, State, Zip:

Billing address (if different):
Address:
Apt, Suite, Bldg, etc:
City, State, Zip:

What service do you need?

☐ Flat surfaces:
Type of material (concrete, pavers, wood, etc.)
If concrete, how old?
Any oil or rust stains we should know about?

☐ House Wash:
Type of material (brick, vinyl, stucco, wood, etc.)
Square footage of home/building:
How many stories?
If cleaning windows, how many?
If cleaning gutters, how old?

☐ Roof Wash:
Type of material (shingle, tile, metal, wood, etc.)
Anything on the roof? (satellite dish, solar panels, etc.)

☐ Do you have a running water hookup onsite for a water hose?
☐ Does anything need to be moved? (cars, furniture, plants, decorations, etc.) If we are responsible for moving items and putting them back, we may charge a fee.
☐ Do you have any pets? Inform pet owners they should keep pets indoors or away from work area until everything is dry. If pet safe products are preferred, there will be an upcharge and deposit required.
☐ Do you live on/near any bodies of water? (lake, river, etc.)
☐ Do I need a gate code to access the property?

Best day/time for service
Estimate: $
Notes:

_____
_____
_____
_____
_____

Date:
Name (first & last):
Email Address:
Mobile Phone Number:
Preferred contact method (call, text, email)
How did you hear about us? (Facebook, Google, flyer, friend, etc.)

Property address:	Billing address (if different):
Address:	Address:
Apt, Suite, Bldg, etc:	Apt, Suite, Bldg, etc:
City, State, Zip:	City, State, Zip:

What service do you need?

☐ Flat surfaces:
Type of material (concrete, pavers, wood, etc.)
If concrete, how old?
Any oil or rust stains we should know about?

☐ House Wash:
Type of material (brick, vinyl, stucco, wood, etc.)
Square footage of home/building:
How many stories?
If cleaning windows, how many?
If cleaning gutters, how old?

☐ Roof Wash:
Type of material (shingle, tile, metal, wood, etc.)
Anything on the roof? (satellite dish, solar panels, etc.)

☐ Do you have a running water hookup onsite for a water hose?
☐ Does anything need to be moved? (cars, furniture, plants, decorations, etc.) If we are responsible for moving items and putting them back, we may charge a fee.
☐ Do you have any pets? Inform pet owners they should keep pets indoors or away from work area until everything is dry. If pet safe products are preferred, there will be an upcharge and deposit required.
☐ Do you live on/near any bodies of water? (lake, river, etc.)
☐ Do I need a gate code to access the property?

Best day/time for service
Estimate: $
Notes:
_____
_____
_____
_____

Date:
Name (first & last):
Email Address:
Mobile Phone Number:
Preferred contact method (call, text, email)
How did you hear about us? (Facebook, Google, flyer, friend, etc.)

Property address:	Billing address (if different):
Address:	Address:
Apt, Suite, Bldg, etc:	Apt, Suite, Bldg, etc:
City, State, Zip:	City, State, Zip:

What service do you need?

☐ Flat surfaces:
Type of material (concrete, pavers, wood, etc.)
If concrete, how old?
Any oil or rust stains we should know about?

☐ House Wash:
Type of material (brick, vinyl, stucco, wood, etc.)
Square footage of home/building:
How many stories?
If cleaning windows, how many?
If cleaning gutters, how old?

☐ Roof Wash:
Type of material (shingle, tile, metal, wood, etc.)
Anything on the roof? (satellite dish, solar panels, etc.)

☐ Do you have a running water hookup onsite for a water hose?
☐ Does anything need to be moved? (cars, furniture, plants, decorations, etc.) If we are responsible for moving items and putting them back, we may charge a fee.
☐ Do you have any pets? Inform pet owners they should keep pets indoors or away from work area until everything is dry. If pet safe products are preferred, there will be an upcharge and deposit required.
☐ Do you live on/near any bodies of water? (lake, river, etc.)
☐ Do I need a gate code to access the property?

Best day/time for service
Estimate: $
Notes:
_____
_____
_____
_____
_____

Date:
Name (first & last):
Email Address:
Mobile Phone Number:
Preferred contact method (call, text, email)
How did you hear about us? (Facebook, Google, flyer, friend, etc.)

Property address: Billing address (if different):
Address: Address:
Apt, Suite, Bldg, etc: Apt, Suite, Bldg, etc:
City, State, Zip: City, State, Zip:

What service do you need?

☐ Flat surfaces:
Type of material (concrete, pavers, wood, etc.)
If concrete, how old?
Any oil or rust stains we should know about?

☐ House Wash:
Type of material (brick, vinyl, stucco, wood, etc.)
Square footage of home/building:
How many stories?
If cleaning windows, how many?
If cleaning gutters, how old?

☐ Roof Wash:
Type of material (shingle, tile, metal, wood, etc.)
Anything on the roof? (satellite dish, solar panels, etc.)

☐ Do you have a running water hookup onsite for a water hose?
☐ Does anything need to be moved? (cars, furniture, plants, decorations, etc.) If we are responsible for moving items and putting them back, we may charge a fee.
☐ Do you have any pets? Inform pet owners they should keep pets indoors or away from work area until everything is dry. If pet safe products are preferred, there will be an upcharge and deposit required.
☐ Do you live on/near any bodies of water? (lake, river, etc.)
☐ Do I need a gate code to access the property?

Best day/time for service
Estimate: $
Notes:
_____
_____
_____
_____

Date:
Name (first & last):
Email Address:
Mobile Phone Number:
Preferred contact method (call, text, email)
How did you hear about us? (Facebook, Google, flyer, friend, etc.)

Property address:
Address:
Apt, Suite, Bldg, etc:
City, State, Zip:

Billing address (if different):
Address:
Apt, Suite, Bldg, etc:
City, State, Zip:

What service do you need?

☐ Flat surfaces:
Type of material (concrete, pavers, wood, etc.)
If concrete, how old?
Any oil or rust stains we should know about?

☐ House Wash:
Type of material (brick, vinyl, stucco, wood, etc.)
Square footage of home/building:
How many stories?
If cleaning windows, how many?
If cleaning gutters, how old?

☐ Roof Wash:
Type of material (shingle, tile, metal, wood, etc.)
Anything on the roof? (satellite dish, solar panels, etc.)

☐ Do you have a running water hookup onsite for a water hose?
☐ Does anything need to be moved? (cars, furniture, plants, decorations, etc.) If we are responsible for moving items and putting them back, we may charge a fee.
☐ Do you have any pets? Inform pet owners they should keep pets indoors or away from work area until everything is dry. If pet safe products are preferred, there will be an upcharge and deposit required.
☐ Do you live on/near any bodies of water? (lake, river, etc.)
☐ Do I need a gate code to access the property?

Best day/time for service
Estimate: $
Notes:

_____
_____
_____
_____
_____

Date:
Name (first & last):
Email Address:
Mobile Phone Number:
Preferred contact method (call, text, email)
How did you hear about us? (Facebook, Google, flyer, friend, etc.)

Property address:	Billing address (if different):
Address:	Address:
Apt, Suite, Bldg, etc:	Apt, Suite, Bldg, etc:
City, State, Zip:	City, State, Zip:

What service do you need?

☐ Flat surfaces:
Type of material (concrete, pavers, wood, etc.)
If concrete, how old?
Any oil or rust stains we should know about?

☐ House Wash:
Type of material (brick, vinyl, stucco, wood, etc.)
Square footage of home/building:
How many stories?
If cleaning windows, how many?
If cleaning gutters, how old?

☐ Roof Wash:
Type of material (shingle, tile, metal, wood, etc.)
Anything on the roof? (satellite dish, solar panels, etc.)

☐ Do you have a running water hookup onsite for a water hose?
☐ Does anything need to be moved? (cars, furniture, plants, decorations, etc.) If we are responsible for moving items and putting them back, we may charge a fee.
☐ Do you have any pets? Inform pet owners they should keep pets indoors or away from work area until everything is dry. If pet safe products are preferred, there will be an upcharge and deposit required.
☐ Do you live on/near any bodies of water? (lake, river, etc.)
☐ Do I need a gate code to access the property?

Best day/time for service
Estimate: $
Notes:
_____
_____
_____
_____

Date:
Name (first & last):
Email Address:
Mobile Phone Number:
Preferred contact method (call, text, email)
How did you hear about us? (Facebook, Google, flyer, friend, etc.)

Property address:
Address:
Apt, Suite, Bldg, etc:
City, State, Zip:

Billing address (if different):
Address:
Apt, Suite, Bldg, etc:
City, State, Zip:

What service do you need?

☐ Flat surfaces:
Type of material (concrete, pavers, wood, etc.)
If concrete, how old?
Any oil or rust stains we should know about?

☐ House Wash:
Type of material (brick, vinyl, stucco, wood, etc.)
Square footage of home/building:
How many stories?
If cleaning windows, how many?
If cleaning gutters, how old?

☐ Roof Wash:
Type of material (shingle, tile, metal, wood, etc.)
Anything on the roof? (satellite dish, solar panels, etc.)

☐ Do you have a running water hookup onsite for a water hose?
☐ Does anything need to be moved? (cars, furniture, plants, decorations, etc.) If we are responsible for moving items and putting them back, we may charge a fee.
☐ Do you have any pets? Inform pet owners they should keep pets indoors or away from work area until everything is dry. If pet safe products are preferred, there will be an upcharge and deposit required.
☐ Do you live on/near any bodies of water? (lake, river, etc.)
☐ Do I need a gate code to access the property?

Best day/time for service
Estimate: $
Notes:

_____
_____
_____
_____
_____

Date:
Name (first & last):
Email Address:
Mobile Phone Number:
Preferred contact method (call, text, email)
How did you hear about us? (Facebook, Google, flyer, friend, etc.)

Property address:	Billing address (if different):
Address:	Address:
Apt, Suite, Bldg, etc:	Apt, Suite, Bldg, etc:
City, State, Zip:	City, State, Zip:

What service do you need?

☐ Flat surfaces:
Type of material (concrete, pavers, wood, etc.)
If concrete, how old?
Any oil or rust stains we should know about?

☐ House Wash:
Type of material (brick, vinyl, stucco, wood, etc.)
Square footage of home/building:
How many stories?
If cleaning windows, how many?
If cleaning gutters, how old?

☐ Roof Wash:
Type of material (shingle, tile, metal, wood, etc.)
Anything on the roof? (satellite dish, solar panels, etc.)

☐ Do you have a running water hookup onsite for a water hose?
☐ Does anything need to be moved? (cars, furniture, plants, decorations, etc.) If we are responsible for moving items and putting them back, we may charge a fee.
☐ Do you have any pets? Inform pet owners they should keep pets indoors or away from work area until everything is dry. If pet safe products are preferred, there will be an upcharge and deposit required.
☐ Do you live on/near any bodies of water? (lake, river, etc.)
☐ Do I need a gate code to access the property?

Best day/time for service
Estimate: $
Notes:
_____
_____
_____
_____

Date:
Name (first & last):
Email Address:
Mobile Phone Number:
Preferred contact method (call, text, email)
How did you hear about us? (Facebook, Google, flyer, friend, etc.)

Property address: Billing address (if different):
Address: Address:
Apt, Suite, Bldg, etc: Apt, Suite, Bldg, etc:
City, State, Zip: City, State, Zip:

What service do you need?

☐ Flat surfaces:
Type of material (concrete, pavers, wood, etc.)
If concrete, how old?
Any oil or rust stains we should know about?

☐ House Wash:
Type of material (brick, vinyl, stucco, wood, etc.)
Square footage of home/building:
How many stories?
If cleaning windows, how many?
If cleaning gutters, how old?

☐ Roof Wash:
Type of material (shingle, tile, metal, wood, etc.)
Anything on the roof? (satellite dish, solar panels, etc.)

☐ Do you have a running water hookup onsite for a water hose?
☐ Does anything need to be moved? (cars, furniture, plants, decorations, etc.) If we are responsible for moving items and putting them back, we may charge a fee.
☐ Do you have any pets? Inform pet owners they should keep pets indoors or away from work area until everything is dry. If pet safe products are preferred, there will be an upcharge and deposit required.
☐ Do you live on/near any bodies of water? (lake, river, etc.)
☐ Do I need a gate code to access the property?

Best day/time for service
Estimate: $
Notes:

_____
_____
_____
_____
_____

Date:
Name (first & last):
Email Address:
Mobile Phone Number:
Preferred contact method (call, text, email)
How did you hear about us? (Facebook, Google, flyer, friend, etc.)

Property address:	Billing address (if different):
Address:	Address:
Apt, Suite, Bldg, etc:	Apt, Suite, Bldg, etc:
City, State, Zip:	City, State, Zip:

What service do you need?

☐ Flat surfaces:
Type of material (concrete, pavers, wood, etc.)
If concrete, how old?
Any oil or rust stains we should know about?

☐ House Wash:
Type of material (brick, vinyl, stucco, wood, etc.)
Square footage of home/building:
How many stories?
If cleaning windows, how many?
If cleaning gutters, how old?

☐ Roof Wash:
Type of material (shingle, tile, metal, wood, etc.)
Anything on the roof? (satellite dish, solar panels, etc.)

☐ Do you have a running water hookup onsite for a water hose?
☐ Does anything need to be moved? (cars, furniture, plants, decorations, etc.) If we are responsible for moving items and putting them back, we may charge a fee.
☐ Do you have any pets? Inform pet owners they should keep pets indoors or away from work area until everything is dry. If pet safe products are preferred, there will be an upcharge and deposit required.
☐ Do you live on/near any bodies of water? (lake, river, etc.)
☐ Do I need a gate code to access the property?

Best day/time for service
Estimate: $
Notes:

___
___
___
___

Date:
Name (first & last):
Email Address:
Mobile Phone Number:
Preferred contact method (call, text, email)
How did you hear about us? (Facebook, Google, flyer, friend, etc.)

Property address:	Billing address (if different):
Address:	Address:
Apt, Suite, Bldg, etc:	Apt, Suite, Bldg, etc:
City, State, Zip:	City, State, Zip:

What service do you need?

☐ Flat surfaces:
Type of material (concrete, pavers, wood, etc.)
If concrete, how old?
Any oil or rust stains we should know about?

☐ House Wash:
Type of material (brick, vinyl, stucco, wood, etc.)
Square footage of home/building:
How many stories?
If cleaning windows, how many?
If cleaning gutters, how old?

☐ Roof Wash:
Type of material (shingle, tile, metal, wood, etc.)
Anything on the roof? (satellite dish, solar panels, etc.)

☐ Do you have a running water hookup onsite for a water hose?
☐ Does anything need to be moved? (cars, furniture, plants, decorations, etc.) If we are responsible for moving items and putting them back, we may charge a fee.
☐ Do you have any pets? Inform pet owners they should keep pets indoors or away from work area until everything is dry. If pet safe products are preferred, there will be an upcharge and deposit required.
☐ Do you live on/near any bodies of water? (lake, river, etc.)
☐ Do I need a gate code to access the property?

Best day/time for service
Estimate: $
Notes:

_____
_____
_____
_____
_____

Date:
Name (first & last):
Email Address:
Mobile Phone Number:
Preferred contact method (call, text, email)
How did you hear about us? (Facebook, Google, flyer, friend, etc.)

Property address:	Billing address (if different):
Address:	Address:
Apt, Suite, Bldg, etc:	Apt, Suite, Bldg, etc:
City, State, Zip:	City, State, Zip:

What service do you need?

☐ Flat surfaces:
Type of material (concrete, pavers, wood, etc.)
If concrete, how old?
Any oil or rust stains we should know about?

☐ House Wash:
Type of material (brick, vinyl, stucco, wood, etc.)
Square footage of home/building:
How many stories?
If cleaning windows, how many?
If cleaning gutters, how old?

☐ Roof Wash:
Type of material (shingle, tile, metal, wood, etc.)
Anything on the roof? (satellite dish, solar panels, etc.)

☐ Do you have a running water hookup onsite for a water hose?
☐ Does anything need to be moved? (cars, furniture, plants, decorations, etc.) If we are responsible for moving items and putting them back, we may charge a fee.
☐ Do you have any pets? Inform pet owners they should keep pets indoors or away from work area until everything is dry. If pet safe products are preferred, there will be an upcharge and deposit required.
☐ Do you live on/near any bodies of water? (lake, river, etc.)
☐ Do I need a gate code to access the property?

Best day/time for service
Estimate: $
Notes:
_____
_____
_____
_____

Date:
Name (first & last):
Email Address:
Mobile Phone Number:
Preferred contact method (call, text, email)
How did you hear about us? (Facebook, Google, flyer, friend, etc.)

Property address: Billing address (if different):
Address: Address:
Apt, Suite, Bldg, etc: Apt, Suite, Bldg, etc:
City, State, Zip: City, State, Zip:

What service do you need?

☐ Flat surfaces:
Type of material (concrete, pavers, wood, etc.)
If concrete, how old?
Any oil or rust stains we should know about?

☐ House Wash:
Type of material (brick, vinyl, stucco, wood, etc.)
Square footage of home/building:
How many stories?
If cleaning windows, how many?
If cleaning gutters, how old?

☐ Roof Wash:
Type of material (shingle, tile, metal, wood, etc.)
Anything on the roof? (satellite dish, solar panels, etc.)

☐ Do you have a running water hookup onsite for a water hose?
☐ Does anything need to be moved? (cars, furniture, plants, decorations, etc.) If we are responsible for moving items and putting them back, we may charge a fee.
☐ Do you have any pets? Inform pet owners they should keep pets indoors or away from work area until everything is dry. If pet safe products are preferred, there will be an upcharge and deposit required.
☐ Do you live on/near any bodies of water? (lake, river, etc.)
☐ Do I need a gate code to access the property?

Best day/time for service
Estimate: $
Notes:

_____
_____
_____
_____
_____

Date:
Name (first & last):
Email Address:
Mobile Phone Number:
Preferred contact method (call, text, email)
How did you hear about us? (Facebook, Google, flyer, friend, etc.)

Property address:	Billing address (if different):
Address:	Address:
Apt, Suite, Bldg, etc:	Apt, Suite, Bldg, etc:
City, State, Zip:	City, State, Zip:

What service do you need?

☐ Flat surfaces:
Type of material (concrete, pavers, wood, etc.)
If concrete, how old?
Any oil or rust stains we should know about?

☐ House Wash:
Type of material (brick, vinyl, stucco, wood, etc.)
Square footage of home/building:
How many stories?
If cleaning windows, how many?
If cleaning gutters, how old?

☐ Roof Wash:
Type of material (shingle, tile, metal, wood, etc.)
Anything on the roof? (satellite dish, solar panels, etc.)

☐ Do you have a running water hookup onsite for a water hose?
☐ Does anything need to be moved? (cars, furniture, plants, decorations, etc.) If we are responsible for moving items and putting them back, we may charge a fee.
☐ Do you have any pets? Inform pet owners they should keep pets indoors or away from work area until everything is dry. If pet safe products are preferred, there will be an upcharge and deposit required.
☐ Do you live on/near any bodies of water? (lake, river, etc.)
☐ Do I need a gate code to access the property?

Best day/time for service
Estimate: $
Notes:
_____
_____
_____
_____

Date:
Name (first & last):
Email Address:
Mobile Phone Number:
Preferred contact method (call, text, email)
How did you hear about us? (Facebook, Google, flyer, friend, etc.)

Property address:	Billing address (if different):
Address:	Address:
Apt, Suite, Bldg, etc:	Apt, Suite, Bldg, etc:
City, State, Zip:	City, State, Zip:

What service do you need?

☐ Flat surfaces:
Type of material (concrete, pavers, wood, etc.)
If concrete, how old?
Any oil or rust stains we should know about?

☐ House Wash:
Type of material (brick, vinyl, stucco, wood, etc.)
Square footage of home/building:
How many stories?
If cleaning windows, how many?
If cleaning gutters, how old?

☐ Roof Wash:
Type of material (shingle, tile, metal, wood, etc.)
Anything on the roof? (satellite dish, solar panels,etc.)

☐ Do you have a running water hookup onsite for a water hose?
☐ Does anything need to be moved? (cars, furniture, plants, decorations, etc.) If we are responsible for moving items and putting them back, we may charge a fee.
☐ Do you have any pets? Inform pet owners they should keep pets indoors or away from work area until everything is dry. If pet safe products are preferred, there will be an upcharge and deposit required.
☐ Do you live on/near any bodies of water? (lake, river, etc.)
☐ Do I need a gate code to access the property?

Best day/time for service
Estimate: $
Notes:
_____
_____
_____
_____
_____

Date:
Name (first & last):
Email Address:
Mobile Phone Number:
Preferred contact method (call, text, email)
How did you hear about us? (Facebook, Google, flyer, friend, etc.)

Property address:	Billing address (if different):
Address:	Address:
Apt, Suite, Bldg, etc:	Apt, Suite, Bldg, etc:
City, State, Zip:	City, State, Zip:

What service do you need?

☐ Flat surfaces:
Type of material (concrete, pavers, wood, etc.)
If concrete, how old?
Any oil or rust stains we should know about?

☐ House Wash:
Type of material (brick, vinyl, stucco, wood, etc.)
Square footage of home/building:
How many stories?
If cleaning windows, how many?
If cleaning gutters, how old?

☐ Roof Wash:
Type of material (shingle, tile, metal, wood, etc.)
Anything on the roof? (satellite dish, solar panels, etc.)

☐ Do you have a running water hookup onsite for a water hose?
☐ Does anything need to be moved? (cars, furniture, plants, decorations, etc.) If we are responsible for moving items and putting them back, we may charge a fee.
☐ Do you have any pets? Inform pet owners they should keep pets indoors or away from work area until everything is dry. If pet safe products are preferred, there will be an upcharge and deposit required.
☐ Do you live on/near any bodies of water? (lake, river, etc.)
☐ Do I need a gate code to access the property?

Best day/time for service
Estimate: $
Notes:
_____
_____
_____
_____

Date:
Name (first & last):
Email Address:
Mobile Phone Number:
Preferred contact method (call, text, email)
How did you hear about us? (Facebook, Google, flyer, friend, etc.)

Property address:	Billing address (if different):
Address:	Address:
Apt, Suite, Bldg, etc:	Apt, Suite, Bldg, etc:
City, State, Zip:	City, State, Zip:

What service do you need?

☐ Flat surfaces:
Type of material (concrete, pavers, wood, etc.)
If concrete, how old?
Any oil or rust stains we should know about?

☐ House Wash:
Type of material (brick, vinyl, stucco, wood, etc.)
Square footage of home/building:
How many stories?
If cleaning windows, how many?
If cleaning gutters, how old?

☐ Roof Wash:
Type of material (shingle, tile, metal, wood, etc.)
Anything on the roof? (satellite dish, solar panels, etc.)

☐ Do you have a running water hookup onsite for a water hose?
☐ Does anything need to be moved? (cars, furniture, plants, decorations, etc.) If we are responsible for moving items and putting them back, we may charge a fee.
☐ Do you have any pets? Inform pet owners they should keep pets indoors or away from work area until everything is dry. If pet safe products are preferred, there will be an upcharge and deposit required.
☐ Do you live on/near any bodies of water? (lake, river, etc.)
☐ Do I need a gate code to access the property?

Best day/time for service
Estimate: $
Notes:

_____
_____
_____
_____
_____

Date:
Name (first & last):
Email Address:
Mobile Phone Number:
Preferred contact method (call, text, email)
How did you hear about us? (Facebook, Google, flyer, friend, etc.)

Property address:	Billing address (if different):
Address:	Address:
Apt, Suite, Bldg, etc:	Apt, Suite, Bldg, etc:
City, State, Zip:	City, State, Zip:

What service do you need?

☐ Flat surfaces:
Type of material (concrete, pavers, wood, etc.)
If concrete, how old?
Any oil or rust stains we should know about?

☐ House Wash:
Type of material (brick, vinyl, stucco, wood, etc.)
Square footage of home/building:
How many stories?
If cleaning windows, how many?
If cleaning gutters, how old?

☐ Roof Wash:
Type of material (shingle, tile, metal, wood, etc.)
Anything on the roof? (satellite dish, solar panels, etc.)

☐ Do you have a running water hookup onsite for a water hose?
☐ Does anything need to be moved? (cars, furniture, plants, decorations, etc.) If we are responsible for moving items and putting them back, we may charge a fee.
☐ Do you have any pets? Inform pet owners they should keep pets indoors or away from work area until everything is dry. If pet safe products are preferred, there will be an upcharge and deposit required.
☐ Do you live on/near any bodies of water? (lake, river, etc.)
☐ Do I need a gate code to access the property?

Best day/time for service
Estimate: $
Notes:
_____
_____
_____
_____

Date:
Name (first & last):
Email Address:
Mobile Phone Number:
Preferred contact method (call, text, email)
How did you hear about us? (Facebook, Google, flyer, friend, etc.)

Property address:	Billing address (if different):
Address:	Address:
Apt, Suite, Bldg, etc:	Apt, Suite, Bldg, etc:
City, State, Zip:	City, State, Zip:

What service do you need?

☐ Flat surfaces:
Type of material (concrete, pavers, wood, etc.)
If concrete, how old?
Any oil or rust stains we should know about?

☐ House Wash:
Type of material (brick, vinyl, stucco, wood, etc.)
Square footage of home/building:
How many stories?
If cleaning windows, how many?
If cleaning gutters, how old?

☐ Roof Wash:
Type of material (shingle, tile, metal, wood, etc.)
Anything on the roof? (satellite dish, solar panels, etc.)

☐ Do you have a running water hookup onsite for a water hose?
☐ Does anything need to be moved? (cars, furniture, plants, decorations, etc.) If we are responsible for moving items and putting them back, we may charge a fee.
☐ Do you have any pets? Inform pet owners they should keep pets indoors or away from work area until everything is dry. If pet safe products are preferred, there will be an upcharge and deposit required.
☐ Do you live on/near any bodies of water? (lake, river, etc.)
☐ Do I need a gate code to access the property?

Best day/time for service
Estimate: $
Notes:
_____
_____
_____
_____
_____

Date:
Name (first & last):
Email Address:
Mobile Phone Number:
Preferred contact method (call, text, email)
How did you hear about us? (Facebook, Google, flyer, friend, etc.)

Property address:	Billing address (if different):
Address:	Address:
Apt, Suite, Bldg, etc:	Apt, Suite, Bldg, etc:
City, State, Zip:	City, State, Zip:

What service do you need?

☐ Flat surfaces:
Type of material (concrete, pavers, wood, etc.)
If concrete, how old?
Any oil or rust stains we should know about?

☐ House Wash:
Type of material (brick, vinyl, stucco, wood, etc.)
Square footage of home/building:
How many stories?
If cleaning windows, how many?
If cleaning gutters, how old?

☐ Roof Wash:
Type of material (shingle, tile, metal, wood, etc.)
Anything on the roof? (satellite dish, solar panels, etc.)

☐ Do you have a running water hookup onsite for a water hose?
☐ Does anything need to be moved? (cars, furniture, plants, decorations, etc.) If we are responsible for moving items and putting them back, we may charge a fee.
☐ Do you have any pets? Inform pet owners they should keep pets indoors or away from work area until everything is dry. If pet safe products are preferred, there will be an upcharge and deposit required.
☐ Do you live on/near any bodies of water? (lake, river, etc.)
☐ Do I need a gate code to access the property?

Best day/time for service
Estimate: $
Notes:
_____
_____
_____
_____

Date:
Name (first & last):
Email Address:
Mobile Phone Number:
Preferred contact method (call, text, email)
How did you hear about us? (Facebook, Google, flyer, friend, etc.)

Property address:
Address:
Apt, Suite, Bldg, etc:
City, State, Zip:

Billing address (if different):
Address:
Apt, Suite, Bldg, etc:
City, State, Zip:

What service do you need?

☐ Flat surfaces:
Type of material (concrete, pavers, wood, etc.)
If concrete, how old?
Any oil or rust stains we should know about?

☐ House Wash:
Type of material (brick, vinyl, stucco, wood, etc.)
Square footage of home/building:
How many stories?
If cleaning windows, how many?
If cleaning gutters, how old?

☐ Roof Wash:
Type of material (shingle, tile, metal, wood, etc.)
Anything on the roof? (satellite dish, solar panels, etc.)

☐ Do you have a running water hookup onsite for a water hose?
☐ Does anything need to be moved? (cars, furniture, plants, decorations, etc.) If we are responsible for moving items and putting them back, we may charge a fee.
☐ Do you have any pets? Inform pet owners they should keep pets indoors or away from work area until everything is dry. If pet safe products are preferred, there will be an upcharge and deposit required.
☐ Do you live on/near any bodies of water? (lake, river, etc.)
☐ Do I need a gate code to access the property?

Best day/time for service
Estimate: $
Notes:

_____
_____
_____
_____
_____

Date:
Name (first & last):
Email Address:
Mobile Phone Number:
Preferred contact method (call, text, email)
How did you hear about us? (Facebook, Google, flyer, friend, etc.)

Property address: Billing address (if different):
Address: Address:
Apt, Suite, Bldg, etc: Apt, Suite, Bldg, etc:
City, State, Zip: City, State, Zip:

What service do you need?

☐ Flat surfaces:
Type of material (concrete, pavers, wood, etc.)
If concrete, how old?
Any oil or rust stains we should know about?

☐ House Wash:
Type of material (brick, vinyl, stucco, wood, etc.)
Square footage of home/building:
How many stories?
If cleaning windows, how many?
If cleaning gutters, how old?

☐ Roof Wash:
Type of material (shingle, tile, metal, wood, etc.)
Anything on the roof? (satellite dish, solar panels,etc.)

☐ Do you have a running water hookup onsite for a water hose?
☐ Does anything need to be moved? (cars, furniture, plants, decorations, etc.) If we are responsible for moving items and putting them back, we may charge a fee.
☐ Do you have any pets? Inform pet owners they should keep pets indoors or away from work area until everything is dry. If pet safe products are preferred, there will be an upcharge and deposit required.
☐ Do you live on/near any bodies of water? (lake, river, etc.)
☐ Do I need a gate code to access the property?

Best day/time for service
Estimate: $
Notes:
_____
_____
_____
_____

Date:
Name (first & last):
Email Address:
Mobile Phone Number:
Preferred contact method (call, text, email)
How did you hear about us? (Facebook, Google, flyer, friend, etc.)

Property address:	Billing address (if different):
Address:	Address:
Apt, Suite, Bldg, etc:	Apt, Suite, Bldg, etc:
City, State, Zip:	City, State, Zip:

What service do you need?

☐ Flat surfaces:
Type of material (concrete, pavers, wood, etc.)
If concrete, how old?
Any oil or rust stains we should know about?

☐ House Wash:
Type of material (brick, vinyl, stucco, wood, etc.)
Square footage of home/building:
How many stories?
If cleaning windows, how many?
If cleaning gutters, how old?

☐ Roof Wash:
Type of material (shingle, tile, metal, wood, etc.)
Anything on the roof? (satellite dish, solar panels, etc.)

☐ Do you have a running water hookup onsite for a water hose?
☐ Does anything need to be moved? (cars, furniture, plants, decorations, etc.) If we are responsible for moving items and putting them back, we may charge a fee.
☐ Do you have any pets? Inform pet owners they should keep pets indoors or away from work area until everything is dry. If pet safe products are preferred, there will be an upcharge and deposit required.
☐ Do you live on/near any bodies of water? (lake, river, etc.)
☐ Do I need a gate code to access the property?

Best day/time for service
Estimate: $
Notes:

_____
_____
_____
_____
_____

Date:
Name (first & last):
Email Address:
Mobile Phone Number:
Preferred contact method (call, text, email)
How did you hear about us? (Facebook, Google, flyer, friend, etc.)

Property address: Billing address (if different):
Address: Address:
Apt, Suite, Bldg, etc: Apt, Suite, Bldg, etc:
City, State, Zip: City, State, Zip:

What service do you need?

☐ Flat surfaces:
Type of material (concrete, pavers, wood, etc.)
If concrete, how old?
Any oil or rust stains we should know about?

☐ House Wash:
Type of material (brick, vinyl, stucco, wood, etc.)
Square footage of home/building:
How many stories?
If cleaning windows, how many?
If cleaning gutters, how old?

☐ Roof Wash:
Type of material (shingle, tile, metal, wood, etc.)
Anything on the roof? (satellite dish, solar panels, etc.)

☐ Do you have a running water hookup onsite for a water hose?
☐ Does anything need to be moved? (cars, furniture, plants, decorations, etc.) If we are responsible for moving items and putting them back, we may charge a fee.
☐ Do you have any pets? Inform pet owners they should keep pets indoors or away from work area until everything is dry. If pet safe products are preferred, there will be an upcharge and deposit required.
☐ Do you live on/near any bodies of water? (lake, river, etc.)
☐ Do I need a gate code to access the property?

Best day/time for service
Estimate: $
Notes:
_____
_____
_____
_____

Date:
Name (first & last):
Email Address:
Mobile Phone Number:
Preferred contact method (call, text, email)
How did you hear about us? (Facebook, Google, flyer, friend, etc.)

Property address:							Billing address (if different):
Address:								Address:
Apt, Suite, Bldg, etc:						Apt, Suite, Bldg, etc:
City, State, Zip:							City, State, Zip:

What service do you need?

☐ Flat surfaces:
Type of material (concrete, pavers, wood, etc.)
If concrete, how old?
Any oil or rust stains we should know about?

☐ House Wash:
Type of material (brick, vinyl, stucco, wood, etc.)
Square footage of home/building:
How many stories?
If cleaning windows, how many?
If cleaning gutters, how old?

☐ Roof Wash:
Type of material (shingle, tile, metal, wood, etc.)
Anything on the roof? (satellite dish, solar panels, etc.)

☐ Do you have a running water hookup onsite for a water hose?
☐ Does anything need to be moved? (cars, furniture, plants, decorations, etc.) If we are responsible for moving items and putting them back, we may charge a fee.
☐ Do you have any pets? Inform pet owners they should keep pets indoors or away from work area until everything is dry. If pet safe products are preferred, there will be an upcharge and deposit required.
☐ Do you live on/near any bodies of water? (lake, river, etc.)
☐ Do I need a gate code to access the property?

Best day/time for service
Estimate: $
Notes:

_____
_____
_____
_____
_____

Date:
Name (first & last):
Email Address:
Mobile Phone Number:
Preferred contact method (call, text, email)
How did you hear about us? (Facebook, Google, flyer, friend, etc.)

Property address: Billing address (if different):
Address: Address:
Apt, Suite, Bldg, etc: Apt, Suite, Bldg, etc:
City, State, Zip: City, State, Zip:

What service do you need?

☐ Flat surfaces:
Type of material (concrete, pavers, wood, etc.)
If concrete, how old?
Any oil or rust stains we should know about?

☐ House Wash:
Type of material (brick, vinyl, stucco, wood, etc.)
Square footage of home/building:
How many stories?
If cleaning windows, how many?
If cleaning gutters, how old?

☐ Roof Wash:
Type of material (shingle, tile, metal, wood, etc.)
Anything on the roof? (satellite dish, solar panels, etc.)

☐ Do you have a running water hookup onsite for a water hose?
☐ Does anything need to be moved? (cars, furniture, plants, decorations, etc.) If we are responsible for moving items and putting them back, we may charge a fee.
☐ Do you have any pets? Inform pet owners they should keep pets indoors or away from work area until everything is dry. If pet safe products are preferred, there will be an upcharge and deposit required.
☐ Do you live on/near any bodies of water? (lake, river, etc.)
☐ Do I need a gate code to access the property?

Best day/time for service
Estimate: $
Notes:
_____
_____
_____
_____

Date:
Name (first & last):
Email Address:
Mobile Phone Number:
Preferred contact method (call, text, email)
How did you hear about us? (Facebook, Google, flyer, friend, etc.)

Property address:
Address:
Apt, Suite, Bldg, etc:
City, State, Zip:

Billing address (if different):
Address:
Apt, Suite, Bldg, etc:
City, State, Zip:

What service do you need?

☐ Flat surfaces:
Type of material (concrete, pavers, wood, etc.)
If concrete, how old?
Any oil or rust stains we should know about?

☐ House Wash:
Type of material (brick, vinyl, stucco, wood, etc.)
Square footage of home/building:
How many stories?
If cleaning windows, how many?
If cleaning gutters, how old?

☐ Roof Wash:
Type of material (shingle, tile, metal, wood, etc.)
Anything on the roof? (satellite dish, solar panels, etc.)

☐ Do you have a running water hookup onsite for a water hose?
☐ Does anything need to be moved? (cars, furniture, plants, decorations, etc.) If we are responsible for moving items and putting them back, we may charge a fee.
☐ Do you have any pets? Inform pet owners they should keep pets indoors or away from work area until everything is dry. If pet safe products are preferred, there will be an upcharge and deposit required.
☐ Do you live on/near any bodies of water? (lake, river, etc.)
☐ Do I need a gate code to access the property?

Best day/time for service
Estimate: $
Notes:

_____
_____
_____
_____
_____

Date:
Name (first & last):
Email Address:
Mobile Phone Number:
Preferred contact method (call, text, email)
How did you hear about us? (Facebook, Google, flyer, friend, etc.)

Property address:	Billing address (if different):
Address:	Address:
Apt, Suite, Bldg, etc:	Apt, Suite, Bldg, etc:
City, State, Zip:	City, State, Zip:

What service do you need?

☐ Flat surfaces:
Type of material (concrete, pavers, wood, etc.)
If concrete, how old?
Any oil or rust stains we should know about?

☐ House Wash:
Type of material (brick, vinyl, stucco, wood, etc.)
Square footage of home/building:
How many stories?
If cleaning windows, how many?
If cleaning gutters, how old?

☐ Roof Wash:
Type of material (shingle, tile, metal, wood, etc.)
Anything on the roof? (satellite dish, solar panels, etc.)

☐ Do you have a running water hookup onsite for a water hose?
☐ Does anything need to be moved? (cars, furniture, plants, decorations, etc.) If we are responsible for moving items and putting them back, we may charge a fee.
☐ Do you have any pets? Inform pet owners they should keep pets indoors or away from work area until everything is dry. If pet safe products are preferred, there will be an upcharge and deposit required.
☐ Do you live on/near any bodies of water? (lake, river, etc.)
☐ Do I need a gate code to access the property?

Best day/time for service
Estimate: $
Notes:
_____
_____
_____
_____

Date:
Name (first & last):
Email Address:
Mobile Phone Number:
Preferred contact method (call, text, email)
How did you hear about us? (Facebook, Google, flyer, friend, etc.)

Property address:	Billing address (if different):
Address:	Address:
Apt, Suite, Bldg, etc:	Apt, Suite, Bldg, etc:
City, State, Zip:	City, State, Zip:

What service do you need?

☐ Flat surfaces:
Type of material (concrete, pavers, wood, etc.)
If concrete, how old?
Any oil or rust stains we should know about?

☐ House Wash:
Type of material (brick, vinyl, stucco, wood, etc.)
Square footage of home/building:
How many stories?
If cleaning windows, how many?
If cleaning gutters, how old?

☐ Roof Wash:
Type of material (shingle, tile, metal, wood, etc.)
Anything on the roof? (satellite dish, solar panels, etc.)

☐ Do you have a running water hookup onsite for a water hose?
☐ Does anything need to be moved? (cars, furniture, plants, decorations, etc.) If we are responsible for moving items and putting them back, we may charge a fee.
☐ Do you have any pets? Inform pet owners they should keep pets indoors or away from work area until everything is dry. If pet safe products are preferred, there will be an upcharge and deposit required.
☐ Do you live on/near any bodies of water? (lake, river, etc.)
☐ Do I need a gate code to access the property?

Best day/time for service
Estimate: $
Notes:

_____
_____
_____
_____
_____

Date:
Name (first & last):
Email Address:
Mobile Phone Number:
Preferred contact method (call, text, email)
How did you hear about us? (Facebook, Google, flyer, friend, etc.)

Property address:
Address:
Apt, Suite, Bldg, etc:
City, State, Zip:

Billing address (if different):
Address:
Apt, Suite, Bldg, etc:
City, State, Zip:

What service do you need?

☐ Flat surfaces:
Type of material (concrete, pavers, wood, etc.)
If concrete, how old?
Any oil or rust stains we should know about?

☐ House Wash:
Type of material (brick, vinyl, stucco, wood, etc.)
Square footage of home/building:
How many stories?
If cleaning windows, how many?
If cleaning gutters, how old?

☐ Roof Wash:
Type of material (shingle, tile, metal, wood, etc.)
Anything on the roof? (satellite dish, solar panels, etc.)

☐ Do you have a running water hookup onsite for a water hose?
☐ Does anything need to be moved? (cars, furniture, plants, decorations, etc.) If we are responsible for moving items and putting them back, we may charge a fee.
☐ Do you have any pets? Inform pet owners they should keep pets indoors or away from work area until everything is dry. If pet safe products are preferred, there will be an upcharge and deposit required.
☐ Do you live on/near any bodies of water? (lake, river, etc.)
☐ Do I need a gate code to access the property?

Best day/time for service
Estimate: $
Notes:

_____
_____
_____
_____

Date:
Name (first & last):
Email Address:
Mobile Phone Number:
Preferred contact method (call, text, email)
How did you hear about us? (Facebook, Google, flyer, friend, etc.)

Property address:　　　　　　　　　　　Billing address (if different):
Address:　　　　　　　　　　　　　　　Address:
Apt, Suite, Bldg, etc:　　　　　　　　　Apt, Suite, Bldg, etc:
City, State, Zip:　　　　　　　　　　　 City, State, Zip:

What service do you need?

☐ Flat surfaces:
Type of material (concrete, pavers, wood, etc.)
If concrete, how old?
Any oil or rust stains we should know about?

☐ House Wash:
Type of material (brick, vinyl, stucco, wood, etc.)
Square footage of home/building:
How many stories?
If cleaning windows, how many?
If cleaning gutters, how old?

☐ Roof Wash:
Type of material (shingle, tile, metal, wood, etc.)
Anything on the roof? (satellite dish, solar panels, etc.)

☐ Do you have a running water hookup onsite for a water hose?
☐ Does anything need to be moved? (cars, furniture, plants, decorations, etc.) If we are responsible for moving items and putting them back, we may charge a fee.
☐ Do you have any pets? Inform pet owners they should keep pets indoors or away from work area until everything is dry. If pet safe products are preferred, there will be an upcharge and deposit required.
☐ Do you live on/near any bodies of water? (lake, river, etc.)
☐ Do I need a gate code to access the property?

Best day/time for service
Estimate: $
Notes:
_____
_____
_____
_____
_____

Date:
Name (first & last):
Email Address:
Mobile Phone Number:
Preferred contact method (call, text, email)
How did you hear about us? (Facebook, Google, flyer, friend, etc.)

Property address:	Billing address (if different):
Address:	Address:
Apt, Suite, Bldg, etc:	Apt, Suite, Bldg, etc:
City, State, Zip:	City, State, Zip:

What service do you need?

☐ Flat surfaces:
Type of material (concrete, pavers, wood, etc.)
If concrete, how old?
Any oil or rust stains we should know about?

☐ House Wash:
Type of material (brick, vinyl, stucco, wood, etc.)
Square footage of home/building:
How many stories?
If cleaning windows, how many?
If cleaning gutters, how old?

☐ Roof Wash:
Type of material (shingle, tile, metal, wood, etc.)
Anything on the roof? (satellite dish, solar panels, etc.)

☐ Do you have a running water hookup onsite for a water hose?
☐ Does anything need to be moved? (cars, furniture, plants, decorations, etc.) If we are responsible for moving items and putting them back, we may charge a fee.
☐ Do you have any pets? Inform pet owners they should keep pets indoors or away from work area until everything is dry. If pet safe products are preferred, there will be an upcharge and deposit required.
☐ Do you live on/near any bodies of water? (lake, river, etc.)
☐ Do I need a gate code to access the property?

Best day/time for service
Estimate: $
Notes:
_____
_____
_____
_____

Date:
Name (first & last):
Email Address:
Mobile Phone Number:
Preferred contact method (call, text, email)
How did you hear about us? (Facebook, Google, flyer, friend, etc.)

Property address:	Billing address (if different):
Address:	Address:
Apt, Suite, Bldg, etc:	Apt, Suite, Bldg, etc:
City, State, Zip:	City, State, Zip:

What service do you need?

☐ Flat surfaces:
Type of material (concrete, pavers, wood, etc.)
If concrete, how old?
Any oil or rust stains we should know about?

☐ House Wash:
Type of material (brick, vinyl, stucco, wood, etc.)
Square footage of home/building:
How many stories?
If cleaning windows, how many?
If cleaning gutters, how old?

☐ Roof Wash:
Type of material (shingle, tile, metal, wood, etc.)
Anything on the roof? (satellite dish, solar panels, etc.)

☐ Do you have a running water hookup onsite for a water hose?
☐ Does anything need to be moved? (cars, furniture, plants, decorations, etc.) If we are responsible for moving items and putting them back, we may charge a fee.
☐ Do you have any pets? Inform pet owners they should keep pets indoors or away from work area until everything is dry. If pet safe products are preferred, there will be an upcharge and deposit required.
☐ Do you live on/near any bodies of water? (lake, river, etc.)
☐ Do I need a gate code to access the property?

Best day/time for service
Estimate: $
Notes:

_____
_____
_____
_____
_____

Date:
Name (first & last):
Email Address:
Mobile Phone Number:
Preferred contact method (call, text, email)
How did you hear about us? (Facebook, Google, flyer, friend, etc.)

Property address:	Billing address (if different):
Address:	Address:
Apt, Suite, Bldg, etc:	Apt, Suite, Bldg, etc:
City, State, Zip:	City, State, Zip:

What service do you need?

☐ Flat surfaces:
Type of material (concrete, pavers, wood, etc.)
If concrete, how old?
Any oil or rust stains we should know about?

☐ House Wash:
Type of material (brick, vinyl, stucco, wood, etc.)
Square footage of home/building:
How many stories?
If cleaning windows, how many?
If cleaning gutters, how old?

☐ Roof Wash:
Type of material (shingle, tile, metal, wood, etc.)
Anything on the roof? (satellite dish, solar panels, etc.)

☐ Do you have a running water hookup onsite for a water hose?
☐ Does anything need to be moved? (cars, furniture, plants, decorations, etc.) If we are responsible for moving items and putting them back, we may charge a fee.
☐ Do you have any pets? Inform pet owners they should keep pets indoors or away from work area until everything is dry. If pet safe products are preferred, there will be an upcharge and deposit required.
☐ Do you live on/near any bodies of water? (lake, river, etc.)
☐ Do I need a gate code to access the property?

Best day/time for service
Estimate: $
Notes:
_____
_____
_____
_____

Date:
Name (first & last):
Email Address:
Mobile Phone Number:
Preferred contact method (call, text, email)
How did you hear about us? (Facebook, Google, flyer, friend, etc.)

Property address:	Billing address (if different):
Address:	Address:
Apt, Suite, Bldg, etc:	Apt, Suite, Bldg, etc:
City, State, Zip:	City, State, Zip:

What service do you need?

☐ Flat surfaces:
Type of material (concrete, pavers, wood, etc.)
If concrete, how old?
Any oil or rust stains we should know about?

☐ House Wash:
Type of material (brick, vinyl, stucco, wood, etc.)
Square footage of home/building:
How many stories?
If cleaning windows, how many?
If cleaning gutters, how old?

☐ Roof Wash:
Type of material (shingle, tile, metal, wood, etc.)
Anything on the roof? (satellite dish, solar panels, etc.)

☐ Do you have a running water hookup onsite for a water hose?
☐ Does anything need to be moved? (cars, furniture, plants, decorations, etc.) If we are responsible for moving items and putting them back, we may charge a fee.
☐ Do you have any pets? Inform pet owners they should keep pets indoors or away from work area until everything is dry. If pet safe products are preferred, there will be an upcharge and deposit required.
☐ Do you live on/near any bodies of water? (lake, river, etc.)
☐ Do I need a gate code to access the property?

Best day/time for service
Estimate: $
Notes:

_____
_____
_____
_____
_____

Date:
Name (first & last):
Email Address:
Mobile Phone Number:
Preferred contact method (call, text, email)
How did you hear about us? (Facebook, Google, flyer, friend, etc.)

Property address:	Billing address (if different):
Address:	Address:
Apt, Suite, Bldg, etc:	Apt, Suite, Bldg, etc:
City, State, Zip:	City, State, Zip:

What service do you need?

☐ Flat surfaces:
Type of material (concrete, pavers, wood, etc.)
If concrete, how old?
Any oil or rust stains we should know about?

☐ House Wash:
Type of material (brick, vinyl, stucco, wood, etc.)
Square footage of home/building:
How many stories?
If cleaning windows, how many?
If cleaning gutters, how old?

☐ Roof Wash:
Type of material (shingle, tile, metal, wood, etc.)
Anything on the roof? (satellite dish, solar panels, etc.)

☐ Do you have a running water hookup onsite for a water hose?
☐ Does anything need to be moved? (cars, furniture, plants, decorations, etc.) If we are responsible for moving items and putting them back, we may charge a fee.
☐ Do you have any pets? Inform pet owners they should keep pets indoors or away from work area until everything is dry. If pet safe products are preferred, there will be an upcharge and deposit required.
☐ Do you live on/near any bodies of water? (lake, river, etc.)
☐ Do I need a gate code to access the property?

Best day/time for service
Estimate: $
Notes:
_____
_____
_____
_____

Date:
Name (first & last):
Email Address:
Mobile Phone Number:
Preferred contact method (call, text, email)
How did you hear about us? (Facebook, Google, flyer, friend, etc.)

Property address:	Billing address (if different):
Address:	Address:
Apt, Suite, Bldg, etc:	Apt, Suite, Bldg, etc:
City, State, Zip:	City, State, Zip:

What service do you need?

☐ Flat surfaces:
Type of material (concrete, pavers, wood, etc.)
If concrete, how old?
Any oil or rust stains we should know about?

☐ House Wash:
Type of material (brick, vinyl, stucco, wood, etc.)
Square footage of home/building:
How many stories?
If cleaning windows, how many?
If cleaning gutters, how old?

☐ Roof Wash:
Type of material (shingle, tile, metal, wood, etc.)
Anything on the roof? (satellite dish, solar panels, etc.)

☐ Do you have a running water hookup onsite for a water hose?
☐ Does anything need to be moved? (cars, furniture, plants, decorations, etc.) If we are responsible for moving items and putting them back, we may charge a fee.
☐ Do you have any pets? Inform pet owners they should keep pets indoors or away from work area until everything is dry. If pet safe products are preferred, there will be an upcharge and deposit required.
☐ Do you live on/near any bodies of water? (lake, river, etc.)
☐ Do I need a gate code to access the property?

Best day/time for service
Estimate: $
Notes:

_____
_____
_____
_____
_____

Date:
Name (first & last):
Email Address:
Mobile Phone Number:
Preferred contact method (call, text, email)
How did you hear about us? (Facebook, Google, flyer, friend, etc.)

Property address:	Billing address (if different):
Address:	Address:
Apt, Suite, Bldg, etc:	Apt, Suite, Bldg, etc:
City, State, Zip:	City, State, Zip:

What service do you need?

☐ Flat surfaces:
Type of material (concrete, pavers, wood, etc.)
If concrete, how old?
Any oil or rust stains we should know about?

☐ House Wash:
Type of material (brick, vinyl, stucco, wood, etc.)
Square footage of home/building:
How many stories?
If cleaning windows, how many?
If cleaning gutters, how old?

☐ Roof Wash:
Type of material (shingle, tile, metal, wood, etc.)
Anything on the roof? (satellite dish, solar panels, etc.)

☐ Do you have a running water hookup onsite for a water hose?
☐ Does anything need to be moved? (cars, furniture, plants, decorations, etc.) If we are responsible for moving items and putting them back, we may charge a fee.
☐ Do you have any pets? Inform pet owners they should keep pets indoors or away from work area until everything is dry. If pet safe products are preferred, there will be an upcharge and deposit required.
☐ Do you live on/near any bodies of water? (lake, river, etc.)
☐ Do I need a gate code to access the property?

Best day/time for service
Estimate: $
Notes:
_____
_____
_____
_____

Date:
Name (first & last):
Email Address:
Mobile Phone Number:
Preferred contact method (call, text, email)
How did you hear about us? (Facebook, Google, flyer, friend, etc.)

Property address:	Billing address (if different):
Address:	Address:
Apt, Suite, Bldg, etc:	Apt, Suite, Bldg, etc:
City, State, Zip:	City, State, Zip:

What service do you need?

☐ Flat surfaces:
Type of material (concrete, pavers, wood, etc.)
If concrete, how old?
Any oil or rust stains we should know about?

☐ House Wash:
Type of material (brick, vinyl, stucco, wood, etc.)
Square footage of home/building:
How many stories?
If cleaning windows, how many?
If cleaning gutters, how old?

☐ Roof Wash:
Type of material (shingle, tile, metal, wood, etc.)
Anything on the roof? (satellite dish, solar panels, etc.)

☐ Do you have a running water hookup onsite for a water hose?
☐ Does anything need to be moved? (cars, furniture, plants, decorations, etc.) If we are responsible for moving items and putting them back, we may charge a fee.
☐ Do you have any pets? Inform pet owners they should keep pets indoors or away from work area until everything is dry. If pet safe products are preferred, there will be an upcharge and deposit required.
☐ Do you live on/near any bodies of water? (lake, river, etc.)
☐ Do I need a gate code to access the property?

Best day/time for service
Estimate: $
Notes:

_____
_____
_____
_____
_____

Date:
Name (first & last):
Email Address:
Mobile Phone Number:
Preferred contact method (call, text, email)
How did you hear about us? (Facebook, Google, flyer, friend, etc.)

Property address:	Billing address (if different):
Address:	Address:
Apt, Suite, Bldg, etc:	Apt, Suite, Bldg, etc:
City, State, Zip:	City, State, Zip:

What service do you need?

☐ Flat surfaces:
Type of material (concrete, pavers, wood, etc.)
If concrete, how old?
Any oil or rust stains we should know about?

☐ House Wash:
Type of material (brick, vinyl, stucco, wood, etc.)
Square footage of home/building:
How many stories?
If cleaning windows, how many?
If cleaning gutters, how old?

☐ Roof Wash:
Type of material (shingle, tile, metal, wood, etc.)
Anything on the roof? (satellite dish, solar panels, etc.)

☐ Do you have a running water hookup onsite for a water hose?
☐ Does anything need to be moved? (cars, furniture, plants, decorations, etc.) If we are responsible for moving items and putting them back, we may charge a fee.
☐ Do you have any pets? Inform pet owners they should keep pets indoors or away from work area until everything is dry. If pet safe products are preferred, there will be an upcharge and deposit required.
☐ Do you live on/near any bodies of water? (lake, river, etc.)
☐ Do I need a gate code to access the property?

Best day/time for service
Estimate: $
Notes:
_____
_____
_____
_____

Date:
Name (first & last):
Email Address:
Mobile Phone Number:
Preferred contact method (call, text, email)
How did you hear about us? (Facebook, Google, flyer, friend, etc.)

Property address:	Billing address (if different):
Address:	Address:
Apt, Suite, Bldg, etc:	Apt, Suite, Bldg, etc:
City, State, Zip:	City, State, Zip:

What service do you need?

☐ Flat surfaces:
Type of material (concrete, pavers, wood, etc.)
If concrete, how old?
Any oil or rust stains we should know about?

☐ House Wash:
Type of material (brick, vinyl, stucco, wood, etc.)
Square footage of home/building:
How many stories?
If cleaning windows, how many?
If cleaning gutters, how old?

☐ Roof Wash:
Type of material (shingle, tile, metal, wood, etc.)
Anything on the roof? (satellite dish, solar panels, etc.)

☐ Do you have a running water hookup onsite for a water hose?
☐ Does anything need to be moved? (cars, furniture, plants, decorations, etc.) If we are responsible for moving items and putting them back, we may charge a fee.
☐ Do you have any pets? Inform pet owners they should keep pets indoors or away from work area until everything is dry. If pet safe products are preferred, there will be an upcharge and deposit required.
☐ Do you live on/near any bodies of water? (lake, river, etc.)
☐ Do I need a gate code to access the property?

Best day/time for service
Estimate: $
Notes:
_____
_____
_____
_____
_____

Date:
Name (first & last):
Email Address:
Mobile Phone Number:
Preferred contact method (call, text, email)
How did you hear about us? (Facebook, Google, flyer, friend, etc.)

Property address:	Billing address (if different):
Address:	Address:
Apt, Suite, Bldg, etc:	Apt, Suite, Bldg, etc:
City, State, Zip:	City, State, Zip:

What service do you need?

☐ Flat surfaces:
Type of material (concrete, pavers, wood, etc.)
If concrete, how old?
Any oil or rust stains we should know about?

☐ House Wash:
Type of material (brick, vinyl, stucco, wood, etc.)
Square footage of home/building:
How many stories?
If cleaning windows, how many?
If cleaning gutters, how old?

☐ Roof Wash:
Type of material (shingle, tile, metal, wood, etc.)
Anything on the roof? (satellite dish, solar panels, etc.)

☐ Do you have a running water hookup onsite for a water hose?
☐ Does anything need to be moved? (cars, furniture, plants, decorations, etc.) If we are responsible for moving items and putting them back, we may charge a fee.
☐ Do you have any pets? Inform pet owners they should keep pets indoors or away from work area until everything is dry. If pet safe products are preferred, there will be an upcharge and deposit required.
☐ Do you live on/near any bodies of water? (lake, river, etc.)
☐ Do I need a gate code to access the property?

Best day/time for service
Estimate: $
Notes:
_____
_____
_____
_____

Date:
Name (first & last):
Email Address:
Mobile Phone Number:
Preferred contact method (call, text, email)
How did you hear about us? (Facebook, Google, flyer, friend, etc.)

Property address: Billing address (if different):
Address: Address:
Apt, Suite, Bldg, etc: Apt, Suite, Bldg, etc:
City, State, Zip: City, State, Zip:

What service do you need?

☐ Flat surfaces:
Type of material (concrete, pavers, wood, etc.)
If concrete, how old?
Any oil or rust stains we should know about?

☐ House Wash:
Type of material (brick, vinyl, stucco, wood, etc.)
Square footage of home/building:
How many stories?
If cleaning windows, how many?
If cleaning gutters, how old?

☐ Roof Wash:
Type of material (shingle, tile, metal, wood, etc.)
Anything on the roof? (satellite dish, solar panels, etc.)

☐ Do you have a running water hookup onsite for a water hose?
☐ Does anything need to be moved? (cars, furniture, plants, decorations, etc.) If we are responsible for moving items and putting them back, we may charge a fee.
☐ Do you have any pets? Inform pet owners they should keep pets indoors or away from work area until everything is dry. If pet safe products are preferred, there will be an upcharge and deposit required.
☐ Do you live on/near any bodies of water? (lake, river, etc.)
☐ Do I need a gate code to access the property?

Best day/time for service
Estimate: $
Notes:

_____
_____
_____
_____
_____

Date:
Name (first & last):
Email Address:
Mobile Phone Number:
Preferred contact method (call, text, email)
How did you hear about us? (Facebook, Google, flyer, friend, etc.)

Property address: Billing address (if different):
Address: Address:
Apt, Suite, Bldg, etc: Apt, Suite, Bldg, etc:
City, State, Zip: City, State, Zip:

What service do you need?

☐ Flat surfaces:
Type of material (concrete, pavers, wood, etc.)
If concrete, how old?
Any oil or rust stains we should know about?

☐ House Wash:
Type of material (brick, vinyl, stucco, wood, etc.)
Square footage of home/building:
How many stories?
If cleaning windows, how many?
If cleaning gutters, how old?

☐ Roof Wash:
Type of material (shingle, tile, metal, wood, etc.)
Anything on the roof? (satellite dish, solar panels, etc.)

☐ Do you have a running water hookup onsite for a water hose?
☐ Does anything need to be moved? (cars, furniture, plants, decorations, etc.) If we are responsible for moving items and putting them back, we may charge a fee.
☐ Do you have any pets? Inform pet owners they should keep pets indoors or away from work area until everything is dry. If pet safe products are preferred, there will be an upcharge and deposit required.
☐ Do you live on/near any bodies of water? (lake, river, etc.)
☐ Do I need a gate code to access the property?

Best day/time for service
Estimate: $
Notes:
_____
_____
_____
_____

Date:
Name (first & last):
Email Address:
Mobile Phone Number:
Preferred contact method (call, text, email)
How did you hear about us? (Facebook, Google, flyer, friend, etc.)

Property address:	Billing address (if different):
Address:	Address:
Apt, Suite, Bldg, etc:	Apt, Suite, Bldg, etc:
City, State, Zip:	City, State, Zip:

What service do you need?

☐ Flat surfaces:
Type of material (concrete, pavers, wood, etc.)
If concrete, how old?
Any oil or rust stains we should know about?

☐ House Wash:
Type of material (brick, vinyl, stucco, wood, etc.)
Square footage of home/building:
How many stories?
If cleaning windows, how many?
If cleaning gutters, how old?

☐ Roof Wash:
Type of material (shingle, tile, metal, wood, etc.)
Anything on the roof? (satellite dish, solar panels, etc.)

☐ Do you have a running water hookup onsite for a water hose?
☐ Does anything need to be moved? (cars, furniture, plants, decorations, etc.) If we are responsible for moving items and putting them back, we may charge a fee.
☐ Do you have any pets? Inform pet owners they should keep pets indoors or away from work area until everything is dry. If pet safe products are preferred, there will be an upcharge and deposit required.
☐ Do you live on/near any bodies of water? (lake, river, etc.)
☐ Do I need a gate code to access the property?

Best day/time for service
Estimate: $
Notes:

_____
_____
_____
_____
_____

Date:
Name (first & last):
Email Address:
Mobile Phone Number:
Preferred contact method (call, text, email)
How did you hear about us? (Facebook, Google, flyer, friend, etc.)

Property address: Billing address (if different):
Address: Address:
Apt, Suite, Bldg, etc: Apt, Suite, Bldg, etc:
City, State, Zip: City, State, Zip:

What service do you need?

☐ Flat surfaces:
Type of material (concrete, pavers, wood, etc.)
If concrete, how old?
Any oil or rust stains we should know about?

☐ House Wash:
Type of material (brick, vinyl, stucco, wood, etc.)
Square footage of home/building:
How many stories?
If cleaning windows, how many?
If cleaning gutters, how old?

☐ Roof Wash:
Type of material (shingle, tile, metal, wood, etc.)
Anything on the roof? (satellite dish, solar panels, etc.)

☐ Do you have a running water hookup onsite for a water hose?
☐ Does anything need to be moved? (cars, furniture, plants, decorations, etc.) If we are responsible for moving items and putting them back, we may charge a fee.
☐ Do you have any pets? Inform pet owners they should keep pets indoors or away from work area until everything is dry. If pet safe products are preferred, there will be an upcharge and deposit required.
☐ Do you live on/near any bodies of water? (lake, river, etc.)
☐ Do I need a gate code to access the property?

Best day/time for service
Estimate: $
Notes:
_____
_____
_____
_____

Date:
Name (first & last):
Email Address:
Mobile Phone Number:
Preferred contact method (call, text, email)
How did you hear about us? (Facebook, Google, flyer, friend, etc.)

Property address: Billing address (if different):
Address: Address:
Apt, Suite, Bldg, etc: Apt, Suite, Bldg, etc:
City, State, Zip: City, State, Zip:

What service do you need?

☐ Flat surfaces:
Type of material (concrete, pavers, wood, etc.)
If concrete, how old?
Any oil or rust stains we should know about?

☐ House Wash:
Type of material (brick, vinyl, stucco, wood, etc.)
Square footage of home/building:
How many stories?
If cleaning windows, how many?
If cleaning gutters, how old?

☐ Roof Wash:
Type of material (shingle, tile, metal, wood, etc.)
Anything on the roof? (satellite dish, solar panels,etc.)

☐ Do you have a running water hookup onsite for a water hose?
☐ Does anything need to be moved? (cars, furniture, plants, decorations, etc.) If we are responsible for moving items and putting them back, we may charge a fee.
☐ Do you have any pets? Inform pet owners they should keep pets indoors or away from work area until everything is dry. If pet safe products are preferred, there will be an upcharge and deposit required.
☐ Do you live on/near any bodies of water? (lake, river, etc.)
☐ Do I need a gate code to access the property?

Best day/time for service
Estimate: $
Notes:
_____
_____
_____
_____

Date:
Name (first & last):
Email Address:
Mobile Phone Number:
Preferred contact method (call, text, email)
How did you hear about us? (Facebook, Google, flyer, friend, etc.)

Property address: Billing address (if different):
Address: Address:
Apt, Suite, Bldg, etc: Apt, Suite, Bldg, etc:
City, State, Zip: City, State, Zip:

What service do you need?

☐ Flat surfaces:
Type of material (concrete, pavers, wood, etc.)
If concrete, how old?
Any oil or rust stains we should know about?

☐ House Wash:
Type of material (brick, vinyl, stucco, wood, etc.)
Square footage of home/building:
How many stories?
If cleaning windows, how many?
If cleaning gutters, how old?

☐ Roof Wash:
Type of material (shingle, tile, metal, wood, etc.)
Anything on the roof? (satellite dish, solar panels, etc.)

☐ Do you have a running water hookup onsite for a water hose?
☐ Does anything need to be moved? (cars, furniture, plants, decorations, etc.) If we are responsible for moving items and putting them back, we may charge a fee.
☐ Do you have any pets? Inform pet owners they should keep pets indoors or away from work area until everything is dry. If pet safe products are preferred, there will be an upcharge and deposit required.
☐ Do you live on/near any bodies of water? (lake, river, etc.)
☐ Do I need a gate code to access the property?

Best day/time for service
Estimate: $
Notes:
_____
_____
_____
_____

Date:
Name (first & last):
Email Address:
Mobile Phone Number:
Preferred contact method (call, text, email)
How did you hear about us? (Facebook, Google, flyer, friend, etc.)

Property address: Billing address (if different):
Address: Address:
Apt, Suite, Bldg, etc: Apt, Suite, Bldg, etc:
City, State, Zip: City, State, Zip:

What service do you need?

☐ Flat surfaces:
Type of material (concrete, pavers, wood, etc.)
If concrete, how old?
Any oil or rust stains we should know about?

☐ House Wash:
Type of material (brick, vinyl, stucco, wood, etc.)
Square footage of home/building:
How many stories?
If cleaning windows, how many?
If cleaning gutters, how old?

☐ Roof Wash:
Type of material (shingle, tile, metal, wood, etc.)
Anything on the roof? (satellite dish, solar panels, etc.)

☐ Do you have a running water hookup onsite for a water hose?
☐ Does anything need to be moved? (cars, furniture, plants, decorations, etc.) If we are responsible for moving items and putting them back, we may charge a fee.
☐ Do you have any pets? Inform pet owners they should keep pets indoors or away from work area until everything is dry. If pet safe products are preferred, there will be an upcharge and deposit required.
☐ Do you live on/near any bodies of water? (lake, river, etc.)
☐ Do I need a gate code to access the property?

Best day/time for service
Estimate: $
Notes:

_____
_____
_____
_____

Date:
Name (first & last):
Email Address:
Mobile Phone Number:
Preferred contact method (call, text, email)
How did you hear about us? (Facebook, Google, flyer, friend, etc.)

Property address:	Billing address (if different):
Address:	Address:
Apt, Suite, Bldg, etc:	Apt, Suite, Bldg, etc:
City, State, Zip:	City, State, Zip:

What service do you need?

☐ Flat surfaces:
Type of material (concrete, pavers, wood, etc.)
If concrete, how old?
Any oil or rust stains we should know about?

☐ House Wash:
Type of material (brick, vinyl, stucco, wood, etc.)
Square footage of home/building:
How many stories?
If cleaning windows, how many?
If cleaning gutters, how old?

☐ Roof Wash:
Type of material (shingle, tile, metal, wood, etc.)
Anything on the roof? (satellite dish, solar panels, etc.)

☐ Do you have a running water hookup onsite for a water hose?
☐ Does anything need to be moved? (cars, furniture, plants, decorations, etc.) If we are responsible for moving items and putting them back, we may charge a fee.
☐ Do you have any pets? Inform pet owners they should keep pets indoors or away from work area until everything is dry. If pet safe products are preferred, there will be an upcharge and deposit required.
☐ Do you live on/near any bodies of water? (lake, river, etc.)
☐ Do I need a gate code to access the property?

Best day/time for service
Estimate: $
Notes:
_____
_____
_____
_____

Date:
Name (first & last):
Email Address:
Mobile Phone Number:
Preferred contact method (call, text, email)
How did you hear about us? (Facebook, Google, flyer, friend, etc.)

Property address:	Billing address (if different):
Address:	Address:
Apt, Suite, Bldg, etc:	Apt, Suite, Bldg, etc:
City, State, Zip:	City, State, Zip:

What service do you need?

☐ Flat surfaces:
Type of material (concrete, pavers, wood, etc.)
If concrete, how old?
Any oil or rust stains we should know about?

☐ House Wash:
Type of material (brick, vinyl, stucco, wood, etc.)
Square footage of home/building:
How many stories?
If cleaning windows, how many?
If cleaning gutters, how old?

☐ Roof Wash:
Type of material (shingle, tile, metal, wood, etc.)
Anything on the roof? (satellite dish, solar panels, etc.)

☐ Do you have a running water hookup onsite for a water hose?
☐ Does anything need to be moved? (cars, furniture, plants, decorations, etc.) If we are responsible for moving items and putting them back, we may charge a fee.
☐ Do you have any pets? Inform pet owners they should keep pets indoors or away from work area until everything is dry. If pet safe products are preferred, there will be an upcharge and deposit required.
☐ Do you live on/near any bodies of water? (lake, river, etc.)
☐ Do I need a gate code to access the property?

Best day/time for service
Estimate: $
Notes:

_____
_____
_____
_____
_____

Date:
Name (first & last):
Email Address:
Mobile Phone Number:
Preferred contact method (call, text, email)
How did you hear about us? (Facebook, Google, flyer, friend, etc.)

Property address: Billing address (if different):
Address: Address:
Apt, Suite, Bldg, etc: Apt, Suite, Bldg, etc:
City, State, Zip: City, State, Zip:

What service do you need?

☐ Flat surfaces:
Type of material (concrete, pavers, wood, etc.)
If concrete, how old?
Any oil or rust stains we should know about?

☐ House Wash:
Type of material (brick, vinyl, stucco, wood, etc.)
Square footage of home/building:
How many stories?
If cleaning windows, how many?
If cleaning gutters, how old?

☐ Roof Wash:
Type of material (shingle, tile, metal, wood, etc.)
Anything on the roof? (satellite dish, solar panels, etc.)

☐ Do you have a running water hookup onsite for a water hose?
☐ Does anything need to be moved? (cars, furniture, plants, decorations, etc.) If we are responsible for moving items and putting them back, we may charge a fee.
☐ Do you have any pets? Inform pet owners they should keep pets indoors or away from work area until everything is dry. If pet safe products are preferred, there will be an upcharge and deposit required.
☐ Do you live on/near any bodies of water? (lake, river, etc.)
☐ Do I need a gate code to access the property?

Best day/time for service
Estimate: $
Notes:
_____
_____
_____
_____

Date:
Name (first & last):
Email Address:
Mobile Phone Number:
Preferred contact method (call, text, email)
How did you hear about us? (Facebook, Google, flyer, friend, etc.)

Property address:	Billing address (if different):
Address:	Address:
Apt, Suite, Bldg, etc:	Apt, Suite, Bldg, etc:
City, State, Zip:	City, State, Zip:

What service do you need?

☐ Flat surfaces:
Type of material (concrete, pavers, wood, etc.)
If concrete, how old?
Any oil or rust stains we should know about?

☐ House Wash:
Type of material (brick, vinyl, stucco, wood, etc.)
Square footage of home/building:
How many stories?
If cleaning windows, how many?
If cleaning gutters, how old?

☐ Roof Wash:
Type of material (shingle, tile, metal, wood, etc.)
Anything on the roof? (satellite dish, solar panels, etc.)

☐ Do you have a running water hookup onsite for a water hose?
☐ Does anything need to be moved? (cars, furniture, plants, decorations, etc.) If we are responsible for moving items and putting them back, we may charge a fee.
☐ Do you have any pets? Inform pet owners they should keep pets indoors or away from work area until everything is dry. If pet safe products are preferred, there will be an upcharge and deposit required.
☐ Do you live on/near any bodies of water? (lake, river, etc.)
☐ Do I need a gate code to access the property?

Best day/time for service
Estimate: $
Notes:

_____
_____
_____
_____
_____

Date:
Name (first & last):
Email Address:
Mobile Phone Number:
Preferred contact method (call, text, email)
How did you hear about us? (Facebook, Google, flyer, friend, etc.)

Property address:	Billing address (if different):
Address:	Address:
Apt, Suite, Bldg, etc:	Apt, Suite, Bldg, etc:
City, State, Zip:	City, State, Zip:

What service do you need?

☐ Flat surfaces:
Type of material (concrete, pavers, wood, etc.)
If concrete, how old?
Any oil or rust stains we should know about?

☐ House Wash:
Type of material (brick, vinyl, stucco, wood, etc.)
Square footage of home/building:
How many stories?
If cleaning windows, how many?
If cleaning gutters, how old?

☐ Roof Wash:
Type of material (shingle, tile, metal, wood, etc.)
Anything on the roof? (satellite dish, solar panels, etc.)

☐ Do you have a running water hookup onsite for a water hose?
☐ Does anything need to be moved? (cars, furniture, plants, decorations, etc.) If we are responsible for moving items and putting them back, we may charge a fee.
☐ Do you have any pets? Inform pet owners they should keep pets indoors or away from work area until everything is dry. If pet safe products are preferred, there will be an upcharge and deposit required.
☐ Do you live on/near any bodies of water? (lake, river, etc.)
☐ Do I need a gate code to access the property?

Best day/time for service
Estimate: $
Notes:
_____
_____
_____
_____

Date:
Name (first & last):
Email Address:
Mobile Phone Number:
Preferred contact method (call, text, email)
How did you hear about us? (Facebook, Google, flyer, friend, etc.)

Property address:	Billing address (if different):
Address:	Address:
Apt, Suite, Bldg, etc:	Apt, Suite, Bldg, etc:
City, State, Zip:	City, State, Zip:

What service do you need?

☐ Flat surfaces:
Type of material (concrete, pavers, wood, etc.)
If concrete, how old?
Any oil or rust stains we should know about?

☐ House Wash:
Type of material (brick, vinyl, stucco, wood, etc.)
Square footage of home/building:
How many stories?
If cleaning windows, how many?
If cleaning gutters, how old?

☐ Roof Wash:
Type of material (shingle, tile, metal, wood, etc.)
Anything on the roof? (satellite dish, solar panels, etc.)

☐ Do you have a running water hookup onsite for a water hose?
☐ Does anything need to be moved? (cars, furniture, plants, decorations, etc.) If we are responsible for moving items and putting them back, we may charge a fee.
☐ Do you have any pets? Inform pet owners they should keep pets indoors or away from work area until everything is dry. If pet safe products are preferred, there will be an upcharge and deposit required.
☐ Do you live on/near any bodies of water? (lake, river, etc.)
☐ Do I need a gate code to access the property?

Best day/time for service
Estimate: $
Notes:
_____
_____
_____
_____

Date:
Name (first & last):
Email Address:
Mobile Phone Number:
Preferred contact method (call, text, email)
How did you hear about us? (Facebook, Google, flyer, friend, etc.)

Property address:
Address:
Apt, Suite, Bldg, etc:
City, State, Zip:

Billing address (if different):
Address:
Apt, Suite, Bldg, etc:
City, State, Zip:

What service do you need?

☐ Flat surfaces:
Type of material (concrete, pavers, wood, etc.)
If concrete, how old?
Any oil or rust stains we should know about?

☐ House Wash:
Type of material (brick, vinyl, stucco, wood, etc.)
Square footage of home/building:
How many stories?
If cleaning windows, how many?
If cleaning gutters, how old?

☐ Roof Wash:
Type of material (shingle, tile, metal, wood, etc.)
Anything on the roof? (satellite dish, solar panels, etc.)

☐ Do you have a running water hookup onsite for a water hose?
☐ Does anything need to be moved? (cars, furniture, plants, decorations, etc.) If we are responsible for moving items and putting them back, we may charge a fee.
☐ Do you have any pets? Inform pet owners they should keep pets indoors or away from work area until everything is dry. If pet safe products are preferred, there will be an upcharge and deposit required.
☐ Do you live on/near any bodies of water? (lake, river, etc.)
☐ Do I need a gate code to access the property?

Best day/time for service
Estimate: $
Notes:
_____
_____
_____
_____

Date:
Name (first & last):
Email Address:
Mobile Phone Number:
Preferred contact method (call, text, email)
How did you hear about us? (Facebook, Google, flyer, friend, etc.)

Property address: Billing address (if different):
Address: Address:
Apt, Suite, Bldg, etc: Apt, Suite, Bldg, etc:
City, State, Zip: City, State, Zip:

What service do you need?

☐ Flat surfaces:
Type of material (concrete, pavers, wood, etc.)
If concrete, how old?
Any oil or rust stains we should know about?

☐ House Wash:
Type of material (brick, vinyl, stucco, wood, etc.)
Square footage of home/building:
How many stories?
If cleaning windows, how many?
If cleaning gutters, how old?

☐ Roof Wash:
Type of material (shingle, tile, metal, wood, etc.)
Anything on the roof? (satellite dish, solar panels, etc.)

☐ Do you have a running water hookup onsite for a water hose?
☐ Does anything need to be moved? (cars, furniture, plants, decorations, etc.) If we are responsible for moving items and putting them back, we may charge a fee.
☐ Do you have any pets? Inform pet owners they should keep pets indoors or away from work area until everything is dry. If pet safe products are preferred, there will be an upcharge and deposit required.
☐ Do you live on/near any bodies of water? (lake, river, etc.)
☐ Do I need a gate code to access the property?

Best day/time for service
Estimate: $
Notes:
_____
_____
_____
_____
_____

Date:
Name (first & last):
Email Address:
Mobile Phone Number:
Preferred contact method (call, text, email)
How did you hear about us? (Facebook, Google, flyer, friend, etc.)

Property address:	Billing address (if different):
Address:	Address:
Apt, Suite, Bldg, etc:	Apt, Suite, Bldg, etc:
City, State, Zip:	City, State, Zip:

What service do you need?

☐ Flat surfaces:
Type of material (concrete, pavers, wood, etc.)
If concrete, how old?
Any oil or rust stains we should know about?

☐ House Wash:
Type of material (brick, vinyl, stucco, wood, etc.)
Square footage of home/building:
How many stories?
If cleaning windows, how many?
If cleaning gutters, how old?

☐ Roof Wash:
Type of material (shingle, tile, metal, wood, etc.)
Anything on the roof? (satellite dish, solar panels, etc.)

☐ Do you have a running water hookup onsite for a water hose?
☐ Does anything need to be moved? (cars, furniture, plants, decorations, etc.) If we are responsible for moving items and putting them back, we may charge a fee.
☐ Do you have any pets? Inform pet owners they should keep pets indoors or away from work area until everything is dry. If pet safe products are preferred, there will be an upcharge and deposit required.
☐ Do you live on/near any bodies of water? (lake, river, etc.)
☐ Do I need a gate code to access the property?

Best day/time for service
Estimate: $
Notes:
_____
_____
_____
_____

Date:
Name (first & last):
Email Address:
Mobile Phone Number:
Preferred contact method (call, text, email)
How did you hear about us? (Facebook, Google, flyer, friend, etc.)

Property address:	Billing address (if different):
Address:	Address:
Apt, Suite, Bldg, etc:	Apt, Suite, Bldg, etc:
City, State, Zip:	City, State, Zip:

What service do you need?

☐ Flat surfaces:
Type of material (concrete, pavers, wood, etc.)
If concrete, how old?
Any oil or rust stains we should know about?

☐ House Wash:
Type of material (brick, vinyl, stucco, wood, etc.)
Square footage of home/building:
How many stories?
If cleaning windows, how many?
If cleaning gutters, how old?

☐ Roof Wash:
Type of material (shingle, tile, metal, wood, etc.)
Anything on the roof? (satellite dish, solar panels, etc.)

☐ Do you have a running water hookup onsite for a water hose?
☐ Does anything need to be moved? (cars, furniture, plants, decorations, etc.) If we are responsible for moving items and putting them back, we may charge a fee.
☐ Do you have any pets? Inform pet owners they should keep pets indoors or away from work area until everything is dry. If pet safe products are preferred, there will be an upcharge and deposit required.
☐ Do you live on/near any bodies of water? (lake, river, etc.)
☐ Do I need a gate code to access the property?

Best day/time for service
Estimate: $
Notes:

_____
_____
_____
_____
_____

Date:
Name (first & last):
Email Address:
Mobile Phone Number:
Preferred contact method (call, text, email)
How did you hear about us? (Facebook, Google, flyer, friend, etc.)

Property address:	Billing address (if different):
Address:	Address:
Apt, Suite, Bldg, etc:	Apt, Suite, Bldg, etc:
City, State, Zip:	City, State, Zip:

What service do you need?

☐ Flat surfaces:
Type of material (concrete, pavers, wood, etc.)
If concrete, how old?
Any oil or rust stains we should know about?

☐ House Wash:
Type of material (brick, vinyl, stucco, wood, etc.)
Square footage of home/building:
How many stories?
If cleaning windows, how many?
If cleaning gutters, how old?

☐ Roof Wash:
Type of material (shingle, tile, metal, wood, etc.)
Anything on the roof? (satellite dish, solar panels, etc.)

☐ Do you have a running water hookup onsite for a water hose?
☐ Does anything need to be moved? (cars, furniture, plants, decorations, etc.) If we are responsible for moving items and putting them back, we may charge a fee.
☐ Do you have any pets? Inform pet owners they should keep pets indoors or away from work area until everything is dry. If pet safe products are preferred, there will be an upcharge and deposit required.
☐ Do you live on/near any bodies of water? (lake, river, etc.)
☐ Do I need a gate code to access the property?

Best day/time for service
Estimate: $
Notes:
_____
_____
_____
_____

Date:
Name (first & last):
Email Address:
Mobile Phone Number:
Preferred contact method (call, text, email)
How did you hear about us? (Facebook, Google, flyer, friend, etc.)

Property address:
Address:
Apt, Suite, Bldg, etc:
City, State, Zip:

Billing address (if different):
Address:
Apt, Suite, Bldg, etc:
City, State, Zip:

What service do you need?

☐ Flat surfaces:
Type of material (concrete, pavers, wood, etc.)
If concrete, how old?
Any oil or rust stains we should know about?

☐ House Wash:
Type of material (brick, vinyl, stucco, wood, etc.)
Square footage of home/building:
How many stories?
If cleaning windows, how many?
If cleaning gutters, how old?

☐ Roof Wash:
Type of material (shingle, tile, metal, wood, etc.)
Anything on the roof? (satellite dish, solar panels, etc.)

☐ Do you have a running water hookup onsite for a water hose?
☐ Does anything need to be moved? (cars, furniture, plants, decorations, etc.) If we are responsible for moving items and putting them back, we may charge a fee.
☐ Do you have any pets? Inform pet owners they should keep pets indoors or away from work area until everything is dry. If pet safe products are preferred, there will be an upcharge and deposit required.
☐ Do you live on/near any bodies of water? (lake, river, etc.)
☐ Do I need a gate code to access the property?

Best day/time for service
Estimate: $
Notes:
_____
_____
_____
_____
_____

Date:
Name (first & last):
Email Address:
Mobile Phone Number:
Preferred contact method (call, text, email)
How did you hear about us? (Facebook, Google, flyer, friend, etc.)

Property address:
Address:
Apt, Suite, Bldg, etc:
City, State, Zip:

Billing address (if different):
Address:
Apt, Suite, Bldg, etc:
City, State, Zip:

What service do you need?

☐ Flat surfaces:
Type of material (concrete, pavers, wood, etc.)
If concrete, how old?
Any oil or rust stains we should know about?

☐ House Wash:
Type of material (brick, vinyl, stucco, wood, etc.)
Square footage of home/building:
How many stories?
If cleaning windows, how many?
If cleaning gutters, how old?

☐ Roof Wash:
Type of material (shingle, tile, metal, wood, etc.)
Anything on the roof? (satellite dish, solar panels, etc.)

☐ Do you have a running water hookup onsite for a water hose?
☐ Does anything need to be moved? (cars, furniture, plants, decorations, etc.) If we are responsible for moving items and putting them back, we may charge a fee.
☐ Do you have any pets? Inform pet owners they should keep pets indoors or away from work area until everything is dry. If pet safe products are preferred, there will be an upcharge and deposit required.
☐ Do you live on/near any bodies of water? (lake, river, etc.)
☐ Do I need a gate code to access the property?

Best day/time for service
Estimate: $
Notes:

_____
_____
_____
_____

Date:
Name (first & last):
Email Address:
Mobile Phone Number:
Preferred contact method (call, text, email)
How did you hear about us? (Facebook, Google, flyer, friend, etc.)

Property address:	Billing address (if different):
Address:	Address:
Apt, Suite, Bldg, etc:	Apt, Suite, Bldg, etc:
City, State, Zip:	City, State, Zip:

What service do you need?

☐ Flat surfaces:
Type of material (concrete, pavers, wood, etc.)
If concrete, how old?
Any oil or rust stains we should know about?

☐ House Wash:
Type of material (brick, vinyl, stucco, wood, etc.)
Square footage of home/building:
How many stories?
If cleaning windows, how many?
If cleaning gutters, how old?

☐ Roof Wash:
Type of material (shingle, tile, metal, wood, etc.)
Anything on the roof? (satellite dish, solar panels, etc.)

☐ Do you have a running water hookup onsite for a water hose?
☐ Does anything need to be moved? (cars, furniture, plants, decorations, etc.) If we are responsible for moving items and putting them back, we may charge a fee.
☐ Do you have any pets? Inform pet owners they should keep pets indoors or away from work area until everything is dry. If pet safe products are preferred, there will be an upcharge and deposit required.
☐ Do you live on/near any bodies of water? (lake, river, etc.)
☐ Do I need a gate code to access the property?

Best day/time for service
Estimate: $
Notes:

_____
_____
_____
_____
_____

Date:
Name (first & last):
Email Address:
Mobile Phone Number:
Preferred contact method (call, text, email)
How did you hear about us? (Facebook, Google, flyer, friend, etc.)

Property address: Billing address (if different):
Address: Address:
Apt, Suite, Bldg, etc: Apt, Suite, Bldg, etc:
City, State, Zip: City, State, Zip:

What service do you need?

☐ Flat surfaces:
Type of material (concrete, pavers, wood, etc.)
If concrete, how old?
Any oil or rust stains we should know about?

☐ House Wash:
Type of material (brick, vinyl, stucco, wood, etc.)
Square footage of home/building:
How many stories?
If cleaning windows, how many?
If cleaning gutters, how old?

☐ Roof Wash:
Type of material (shingle, tile, metal, wood, etc.)
Anything on the roof? (satellite dish, solar panels, etc.)

☐ Do you have a running water hookup onsite for a water hose?
☐ Does anything need to be moved? (cars, furniture, plants, decorations, etc.) If we are responsible for moving items and putting them back, we may charge a fee.
☐ Do you have any pets? Inform pet owners they should keep pets indoors or away from work area until everything is dry. If pet safe products are preferred, there will be an upcharge and deposit required.
☐ Do you live on/near any bodies of water? (lake, river, etc.)
☐ Do I need a gate code to access the property?

Best day/time for service
Estimate: $
Notes:
_____
_____
_____
_____

Date:
Name (first & last):
Email Address:
Mobile Phone Number:
Preferred contact method (call, text, email)
How did you hear about us? (Facebook, Google, flyer, friend, etc.)

Property address:	Billing address (if different):
Address:	Address:
Apt, Suite, Bldg, etc:	Apt, Suite, Bldg, etc:
City, State, Zip:	City, State, Zip:

What service do you need?

☐ Flat surfaces:
Type of material (concrete, pavers, wood, etc.)
If concrete, how old?
Any oil or rust stains we should know about?

☐ House Wash:
Type of material (brick, vinyl, stucco, wood, etc.)
Square footage of home/building:
How many stories?
If cleaning windows, how many?
If cleaning gutters, how old?

☐ Roof Wash:
Type of material (shingle, tile, metal, wood, etc.)
Anything on the roof? (satellite dish, solar panels, etc.)

☐ Do you have a running water hookup onsite for a water hose?
☐ Does anything need to be moved? (cars, furniture, plants, decorations, etc.) If we are responsible for moving items and putting them back, we may charge a fee.
☐ Do you have any pets? Inform pet owners they should keep pets indoors or away from work area until everything is dry. If pet safe products are preferred, there will be an upcharge and deposit required.
☐ Do you live on/near any bodies of water? (lake, river, etc.)
☐ Do I need a gate code to access the property?

Best day/time for service
Estimate: $
Notes:

_____
_____
_____
_____
_____

Date:
Name (first & last):
Email Address:
Mobile Phone Number:
Preferred contact method (call, text, email)
How did you hear about us? (Facebook, Google, flyer, friend, etc.)

Property address:	Billing address (if different):
Address:	Address:
Apt, Suite, Bldg, etc:	Apt, Suite, Bldg, etc:
City, State, Zip:	City, State, Zip:

What service do you need?

☐ Flat surfaces:
Type of material (concrete, pavers, wood, etc.)
If concrete, how old?
Any oil or rust stains we should know about?

☐ House Wash:
Type of material (brick, vinyl, stucco, wood, etc.)
Square footage of home/building:
How many stories?
If cleaning windows, how many?
If cleaning gutters, how old?

☐ Roof Wash:
Type of material (shingle, tile, metal, wood, etc.)
Anything on the roof? (satellite dish, solar panels, etc.)

☐ Do you have a running water hookup onsite for a water hose?
☐ Does anything need to be moved? (cars, furniture, plants, decorations, etc.) If we are responsible for moving items and putting them back, we may charge a fee.
☐ Do you have any pets? Inform pet owners they should keep pets indoors or away from work area until everything is dry. If pet safe products are preferred, there will be an upcharge and deposit required.
☐ Do you live on/near any bodies of water? (lake, river, etc.)
☐ Do I need a gate code to access the property?

Best day/time for service
Estimate: $
Notes:
_____
_____
_____
_____

Date:
Name (first & last):
Email Address:
Mobile Phone Number:
Preferred contact method (call, text, email)
How did you hear about us? (Facebook, Google, flyer, friend, etc.)

Property address:
Address:
Apt, Suite, Bldg, etc:
City, State, Zip:

Billing address (if different):
Address:
Apt, Suite, Bldg, etc:
City, State, Zip:

What service do you need?

☐ Flat surfaces:
Type of material (concrete, pavers, wood, etc.)
If concrete, how old?
Any oil or rust stains we should know about?

☐ House Wash:
Type of material (brick, vinyl, stucco, wood, etc.)
Square footage of home/building:
How many stories?
If cleaning windows, how many?
If cleaning gutters, how old?

☐ Roof Wash:
Type of material (shingle, tile, metal, wood, etc.)
Anything on the roof? (satellite dish, solar panels, etc.)

☐ Do you have a running water hookup onsite for a water hose?
☐ Does anything need to be moved? (cars, furniture, plants, decorations, etc.) If we are responsible for moving items and putting them back, we may charge a fee.
☐ Do you have any pets? Inform pet owners they should keep pets indoors or away from work area until everything is dry. If pet safe products are preferred, there will be an upcharge and deposit required.
☐ Do you live on/near any bodies of water? (lake, river, etc.)
☐ Do I need a gate code to access the property?

Best day/time for service
Estimate: $
Notes:

_____
_____
_____
_____
_____

Date:
Name (first & last):
Email Address:
Mobile Phone Number:
Preferred contact method (call, text, email)
How did you hear about us? (Facebook, Google, flyer, friend, etc.)

Property address: Billing address (if different):
Address: Address:
Apt, Suite, Bldg, etc: Apt, Suite, Bldg, etc:
City, State, Zip: City, State, Zip:

What service do you need?

☐ Flat surfaces:
Type of material (concrete, pavers, wood, etc.)
If concrete, how old?
Any oil or rust stains we should know about?

☐ House Wash:
Type of material (brick, vinyl, stucco, wood, etc.)
Square footage of home/building:
How many stories?
If cleaning windows, how many?
If cleaning gutters, how old?

☐ Roof Wash:
Type of material (shingle, tile, metal, wood, etc.)
Anything on the roof? (satellite dish, solar panels, etc.)

☐ Do you have a running water hookup onsite for a water hose?
☐ Does anything need to be moved? (cars, furniture, plants, decorations, etc.) If we are responsible for moving items and putting them back, we may charge a fee.
☐ Do you have any pets? Inform pet owners they should keep pets indoors or away from work area until everything is dry. If pet safe products are preferred, there will be an upcharge and deposit required.
☐ Do you live on/near any bodies of water? (lake, river, etc.)
☐ Do I need a gate code to access the property?

Best day/time for service
Estimate: $
Notes:
_____
_____
_____
_____
_____

Date:
Name (first & last):
Email Address:
Mobile Phone Number:
Preferred contact method (call, text, email)
How did you hear about us? (Facebook, Google, flyer, friend, etc.)

Property address:
Address:
Apt, Suite, Bldg, etc:
City, State, Zip:

Billing address (if different):
Address:
Apt, Suite, Bldg, etc:
City, State, Zip:

What service do you need?

☐ Flat surfaces:
Type of material (concrete, pavers, wood, etc.)
If concrete, how old?
Any oil or rust stains we should know about?

☐ House Wash:
Type of material (brick, vinyl, stucco, wood, etc.)
Square footage of home/building:
How many stories?
If cleaning windows, how many?
If cleaning gutters, how old?

☐ Roof Wash:
Type of material (shingle, tile, metal, wood, etc.)
Anything on the roof? (satellite dish, solar panels, etc.)

☐ Do you have a running water hookup onsite for a water hose?
☐ Does anything need to be moved? (cars, furniture, plants, decorations, etc.) If we are responsible for moving items and putting them back, we may charge a fee.
☐ Do you have any pets? Inform pet owners they should keep pets indoors or away from work area until everything is dry. If pet safe products are preferred, there will be an upcharge and deposit required.
☐ Do you live on/near any bodies of water? (lake, river, etc.)
☐ Do I need a gate code to access the property?

Best day/time for service
Estimate: $
Notes:

_____
_____
_____
_____
_____

Date:
Name (first & last):
Email Address:
Mobile Phone Number:
Preferred contact method (call, text, email)
How did you hear about us? (Facebook, Google, flyer, friend, etc.)

Property address: Billing address (if different):
Address: Address:
Apt, Suite, Bldg, etc: Apt, Suite, Bldg, etc:
City, State, Zip: City, State, Zip:

What service do you need?

☐ Flat surfaces:
Type of material (concrete, pavers, wood, etc.)
If concrete, how old?
Any oil or rust stains we should know about?

☐ House Wash:
Type of material (brick, vinyl, stucco, wood, etc.)
Square footage of home/building:
How many stories?
If cleaning windows, how many?
If cleaning gutters, how old?

☐ Roof Wash:
Type of material (shingle, tile, metal, wood, etc.)
Anything on the roof? (satellite dish, solar panels, etc.)

☐ Do you have a running water hookup onsite for a water hose?
☐ Does anything need to be moved? (cars, furniture, plants, decorations, etc.) If we are responsible for moving items and putting them back, we may charge a fee.
☐ Do you have any pets? Inform pet owners they should keep pets indoors or away from work area until everything is dry. If pet safe products are preferred, there will be an upcharge and deposit required.
☐ Do you live on/near any bodies of water? (lake, river, etc.)
☐ Do I need a gate code to access the property?

Best day/time for service
Estimate: $
Notes:
_____
_____
_____
_____

Date:
Name (first & last):
Email Address:
Mobile Phone Number:
Preferred contact method (call, text, email)
How did you hear about us? (Facebook, Google, flyer, friend, etc.)

Property address:
Address:
Apt, Suite, Bldg, etc:
City, State, Zip:

Billing address (if different):
Address:
Apt, Suite, Bldg, etc:
City, State, Zip:

What service do you need?

☐ Flat surfaces:
Type of material (concrete, pavers, wood, etc.)
If concrete, how old?
Any oil or rust stains we should know about?

☐ House Wash:
Type of material (brick, vinyl, stucco, wood, etc.)
Square footage of home/building:
How many stories?
If cleaning windows, how many?
If cleaning gutters, how old?

☐ Roof Wash:
Type of material (shingle, tile, metal, wood, etc.)
Anything on the roof? (satellite dish, solar panels, etc.)

☐ Do you have a running water hookup onsite for a water hose?
☐ Does anything need to be moved? (cars, furniture, plants, decorations, etc.) If we are responsible for moving items and putting them back, we may charge a fee.
☐ Do you have any pets? Inform pet owners they should keep pets indoors or away from work area until everything is dry. If pet safe products are preferred, there will be an upcharge and deposit required.
☐ Do you live on/near any bodies of water? (lake, river, etc.)
☐ Do I need a gate code to access the property?

Best day/time for service
Estimate: $
Notes:

_____
_____
_____
_____
_____

Date:
Name (first & last):
Email Address:
Mobile Phone Number:
Preferred contact method (call, text, email)
How did you hear about us? (Facebook, Google, flyer, friend, etc.)

Property address:	Billing address (if different):
Address:	Address:
Apt, Suite, Bldg, etc:	Apt, Suite, Bldg, etc:
City, State, Zip:	City, State, Zip:

What service do you need?

☐ Flat surfaces:
Type of material (concrete, pavers, wood, etc.)
If concrete, how old?
Any oil or rust stains we should know about?

☐ House Wash:
Type of material (brick, vinyl, stucco, wood, etc.)
Square footage of home/building:
How many stories?
If cleaning windows, how many?
If cleaning gutters, how old?

☐ Roof Wash:
Type of material (shingle, tile, metal, wood, etc.)
Anything on the roof? (satellite dish, solar panels, etc.)

☐ Do you have a running water hookup onsite for a water hose?
☐ Does anything need to be moved? (cars, furniture, plants, decorations, etc.) If we are responsible for moving items and putting them back, we may charge a fee.
☐ Do you have any pets? Inform pet owners they should keep pets indoors or away from work area until everything is dry. If pet safe products are preferred, there will be an upcharge and deposit required.
☐ Do you live on/near any bodies of water? (lake, river, etc.)
☐ Do I need a gate code to access the property?

Best day/time for service
Estimate: $
Notes:
_____
_____
_____
_____

Date:
Name (first & last):
Email Address:
Mobile Phone Number:
Preferred contact method (call, text, email)
How did you hear about us? (Facebook, Google, flyer, friend, etc.)

Property address:	Billing address (if different):
Address:	Address:
Apt, Suite, Bldg, etc:	Apt, Suite, Bldg, etc:
City, State, Zip:	City, State, Zip:

What service do you need?

☐ Flat surfaces:
Type of material (concrete, pavers, wood, etc.)
If concrete, how old?
Any oil or rust stains we should know about?

☐ House Wash:
Type of material (brick, vinyl, stucco, wood, etc.)
Square footage of home/building:
How many stories?
If cleaning windows, how many?
If cleaning gutters, how old?

☐ Roof Wash:
Type of material (shingle, tile, metal, wood, etc.)
Anything on the roof? (satellite dish, solar panels, etc.)

☐ Do you have a running water hookup onsite for a water hose?
☐ Does anything need to be moved? (cars, furniture, plants, decorations, etc.) If we are responsible for moving items and putting them back, we may charge a fee.
☐ Do you have any pets? Inform pet owners they should keep pets indoors or away from work area until everything is dry. If pet safe products are preferred, there will be an upcharge and deposit required.
☐ Do you live on/near any bodies of water? (lake, river, etc.)
☐ Do I need a gate code to access the property?

Best day/time for service
Estimate: $
Notes:

_____
_____
_____
_____
_____

Date:
Name (first & last):
Email Address:
Mobile Phone Number:
Preferred contact method (call, text, email)
How did you hear about us? (Facebook, Google, flyer, friend, etc.)

Property address: Billing address (if different):
Address: Address:
Apt, Suite, Bldg, etc: Apt, Suite, Bldg, etc:
City, State, Zip: City, State, Zip:

What service do you need?

☐ Flat surfaces:
Type of material (concrete, pavers, wood, etc.)
If concrete, how old?
Any oil or rust stains we should know about?

☐ House Wash:
Type of material (brick, vinyl, stucco, wood, etc.)
Square footage of home/building:
How many stories?
If cleaning windows, how many?
If cleaning gutters, how old?

☐ Roof Wash:
Type of material (shingle, tile, metal, wood, etc.)
Anything on the roof? (satellite dish, solar panels, etc.)

☐ Do you have a running water hookup onsite for a water hose?
☐ Does anything need to be moved? (cars, furniture, plants, decorations, etc.) If we are responsible for moving items and putting them back, we may charge a fee.
☐ Do you have any pets? Inform pet owners they should keep pets indoors or away from work area until everything is dry. If pet safe products are preferred, there will be an upcharge and deposit required.
☐ Do you live on/near any bodies of water? (lake, river, etc.)
☐ Do I need a gate code to access the property?

Best day/time for service
Estimate: $
Notes:
_____
_____
_____
_____

Date:
Name (first & last):
Email Address:
Mobile Phone Number:
Preferred contact method (call, text, email)
How did you hear about us? (Facebook, Google, flyer, friend, etc.)

Property address:	Billing address (if different):
Address:	Address:
Apt, Suite, Bldg, etc:	Apt, Suite, Bldg, etc:
City, State, Zip:	City, State, Zip:

What service do you need?

☐ Flat surfaces:
Type of material (concrete, pavers, wood, etc.)
If concrete, how old?
Any oil or rust stains we should know about?

☐ House Wash:
Type of material (brick, vinyl, stucco, wood, etc.)
Square footage of home/building:
How many stories?
If cleaning windows, how many?
If cleaning gutters, how old?

☐ Roof Wash:
Type of material (shingle, tile, metal, wood, etc.)
Anything on the roof? (satellite dish, solar panels, etc.)

☐ Do you have a running water hookup onsite for a water hose?
☐ Does anything need to be moved? (cars, furniture, plants, decorations, etc.) If we are responsible for moving items and putting them back, we may charge a fee.
☐ Do you have any pets? Inform pet owners they should keep pets indoors or away from work area until everything is dry. If pet safe products are preferred, there will be an upcharge and deposit required.
☐ Do you live on/near any bodies of water? (lake, river, etc.)
☐ Do I need a gate code to access the property?

Best day/time for service
Estimate: $
Notes:

_____
_____
_____
_____
_____

Date:
Name (first & last):
Email Address:
Mobile Phone Number:
Preferred contact method (call, text, email)
How did you hear about us? (Facebook, Google, flyer, friend, etc.)

Property address:	Billing address (if different):
Address:	Address:
Apt, Suite, Bldg, etc:	Apt, Suite, Bldg, etc:
City, State, Zip:	City, State, Zip:

What service do you need?

☐ Flat surfaces:
Type of material (concrete, pavers, wood, etc.)
If concrete, how old?
Any oil or rust stains we should know about?

☐ House Wash:
Type of material (brick, vinyl, stucco, wood, etc.)
Square footage of home/building:
How many stories?
If cleaning windows, how many?
If cleaning gutters, how old?

☐ Roof Wash:
Type of material (shingle, tile, metal, wood, etc.)
Anything on the roof? (satellite dish, solar panels, etc.)

☐ Do you have a running water hookup onsite for a water hose?
☐ Does anything need to be moved? (cars, furniture, plants, decorations, etc.) If we are responsible for moving items and putting them back, we may charge a fee.
☐ Do you have any pets? Inform pet owners they should keep pets indoors or away from work area until everything is dry. If pet safe products are preferred, there will be an upcharge and deposit required.
☐ Do you live on/near any bodies of water? (lake, river, etc.)
☐ Do I need a gate code to access the property?

Best day/time for service
Estimate: $
Notes:
_____
_____
_____
_____

Date:
Name (first & last):
Email Address:
Mobile Phone Number:
Preferred contact method (call, text, email)
How did you hear about us? (Facebook, Google, flyer, friend, etc.)

Property address:
Address:
Apt, Suite, Bldg, etc:
City, State, Zip:

Billing address (if different):
Address:
Apt, Suite, Bldg, etc:
City, State, Zip:

What service do you need?

☐ Flat surfaces:
Type of material (concrete, pavers, wood, etc.)
If concrete, how old?
Any oil or rust stains we should know about?

☐ House Wash:
Type of material (brick, vinyl, stucco, wood, etc.)
Square footage of home/building:
How many stories?
If cleaning windows, how many?
If cleaning gutters, how old?

☐ Roof Wash:
Type of material (shingle, tile, metal, wood, etc.)
Anything on the roof? (satellite dish, solar panels,etc.)

☐ Do you have a running water hookup onsite for a water hose?
☐ Does anything need to be moved? (cars, furniture, plants, decorations, etc.) If we are responsible for moving items and putting them back, we may charge a fee.
☐ Do you have any pets? Inform pet owners they should keep pets indoors or away from work area until everything is dry. If pet safe products are preferred, there will be an upcharge and deposit required.
☐ Do you live on/near any bodies of water? (lake, river, etc.)
☐ Do I need a gate code to access the property?

Best day/time for service
Estimate: $
Notes:

_____
_____
_____
_____
_____

www.ingramcontent.com/pod-product-compliance
Lightning Source LLC
Chambersburg PA
CBHW031533210526
45464CB00014B/2337